The Biblical Seminar
81

First Person

First Person

Essays in Biblical Autobiography

edited by
Philip R. Davies

SHEFFIELD ACADEMIC PRESS
A Continuum imprint
LONDON • NEW YORK

Published by Sheffield Academic Press Ltd
The Tower Building, 11 York Road, London SE1 7NX
370 Lexington Avenue, New York NY 10017-6550

www.SheffieldAcademicPress.com
www.continuumbooks.com

British Library Cataloguing-in-Publication Data

A catalogue record for this book is available from the British Library

Typeset by Sheffield Academic Press
Printed on acid-free paper in Great Britain by The Cromwell Press, Trowbridge, Wiltshire

ISBN 1-84127-245-0 (paperback)
ISBN 1-84127-320-1 (hardback)

CONTENTS

ACKNOWLEDGEMENT AND DEDICATION

Back in 1994, Ulrika Lindblad from Finland sent me a short essay on Susanna, written in the first person. That essay inspired the book that has now appeared eight years later. And so this book is dedicated to Ulrika Lindblad.

ABBREVIATIONS

AB	Anchor Bible
ABD	David Noel Freedman (ed.), *The Anchor Bible Dictionary* (New York: Doubleday, 1992)
BDB	Francis Brown, S.R. Driver and Charles A. Briggs, *A Hebrew and English Lexicon of the Old Testament* (Oxford: Clarendon Press, 1907)
BibInt	*Biblical Interpretation: A Journal of Contemporary Approaches*
BR	*Bible Review*
BWANT	Beiträge zur Wissenschaft vom Alten und Neuen Testament
EvT	*Evangelische Theologie*
ICC	International Critical Commentary
IEJ	*Israel Exploration Journal*
JAAR	*Journal of the American Academy of Religion*
JBL	*Journal of Biblical Literature*
JES	*Journal of Ecumenical Studies*
JSOT	*Journal for the Study of the Old Testament*
JSOTSup	*Journal for the Study of the Old Testament*, Supplement Series
JTS	*Journal of Theological Studies*
NCB	New Century Bible
NEB	*New English Bible*
OTL	Old Testament Library
RSR	*Recherches de science religieuse*
SBLDS	SBL Dissertation Series
SBLSP	SBL Seminar Papers
TQ	*Theologische Quartalschrift*
VT	*Vetus Testamentum*
ZAW	*Zeitschrift für die alttestamentliche Wissenschaft*

LIST OF CONTRIBUTORS

Yairah Amit is a Professor of Biblical Studies at Tel Aviv University, Israel.

Athalya Brenner is Professor of Hebrew Bible/Old Testament at the Faculty of the Humanities, University of Amsterdam, The Netherlands.

Gillian Cooper studied Theology at Oxford, specializing in Old Testament, was ordained, and then taught at St John's College, Nottingham.

John Goldingay studied Theology at Oxford, specializing in Old Testament, was ordained, and then taught at John's College, Nottingham.

Philip Davies is Professor of Biblical Studies at the University of Sheffield and the Editorial Director of Sheffield Academic Press.

Francis Landy is Professor of Religious Studies at the University of Alberta, USA.

Jonathan Magonet is Principal of Leo Baeck College, London, where he lectures in Bible.

Hugh Pyper is Senior Lecturer in Biblical Studies and Head of School in the School of Theology and Religious Studies, University of Leeds, England.

Suzanne Shaw received her M.S. in Marriage and Family Therapy from Fuller Theological Seminary in Pasadena, California, and currently practises Marriage and Family Therapy at La Vie Counseling Center (also in Pasadena).

INTRODUCTION: AUTOBIOGRAPHY AS EXEGESIS

Philip R. Davies

Pseudepigrapha

This book is a collection of modern pseudepigrapha, in other words writings in the name of biblical personages composed by contemporary scholars. Is this quasi-novelistic mode of commentary an appropriate genre for biblical scholarship? Some justification for it might seem warranted. My justification is not necessarily shared by the other contributors, for whom I shall not speak. But each of them readily assented to the commissioned task, and so no doubt they thought such an exercise to be a worthwhile application of biblical scholarship.

My own defence of a volume of biblical autobiography is twofold: first that it resurrects a respected (and learned) ancient mode of biblical exegesis, offering a critical, or even 'post-critical', reworking of a 'pre-critical' tradition; and second, that it represents the application of modern narrative theory, or 'narratology'. Before reviewing the essays in this book, then, let me consider these two aspects of the enterprise.

Ancient Pseudepigraphy

The autobiographical voice is definitely a scriptural one: Deuteronomy itself, as Morton Smith observed (Smith 1971) is a Mosaic pseudepigraphon; then we have the second half of Daniel. Proverbs, the Song of Songs and Ecclesiastes are Solomonic pseudepigraphy (on the rhetorical function of this strategy in Ecclesiastes, see Christianson 1998). Much of the content of the prophetic books too, of course, also puts words into the mouth of eponymous seers. In the late Second Temple period and beyond the Hebrew Bible, pseudepigraphic works proliferate: 1 Enoch is substantially, and the Book of Jubilees entirely, pseudepigraphy, and numerous testaments and apocalypses adorn the major biblical characters from Adam onwards. In the New Testament there are Pauline pseudepigrapha, and perhaps other such epistles also. The fashion for assigning venerable authors to first-person writings not their own also played some part in the process of either canonizing or rationalizing the Jewish and Christian scriptures: thus the Psalms and Lamentations have been *received* as pseudepigrapha.

So we are engaging in a literary game of some importance to the creation and reception of our Bible. The function of the pseudo-autobiographical voice is closely connected in some way with the processes of canonizing, whether by assigning a work to a tradition associated with a person (as in the case of the Mosaic torah or the Enochic corpus) or buttressing the authority of a more rigorously defined religious canon by ascribing the entire contents to reputable scribes (such as Moses, Samuel, Ezra). But do the same motivations hold for the (non-canonized) writings now to be found among the non-biblical Jewish writings that we call 'Pseudepigrapha'? Or was there some other motive for the attribution of such texts to ancient figures? There is, I think, more to this mechanism than the crude desire to impute some spurious authority.

Indeed, were all these ascriptions really *deceptive*? Do we moderns overestimate the gullibility of ancient readers by even raising that question? Arguments can be made on both sides. Josephus at any rate allowed himself to be taken in by at least the biblical attributions. Yet Porphyry was not taken in by Daniel—even if the author of Daniel intended him to be, which we cannot tell. The contemporary Hellenistic schools and libraries were well aware of the question of authenticity and devoted much research to it. Was pseudepigraphy a genre that the author expected to be recognized by competent readers and its transparent fictionality enjoyed for itself? How far did such works intend to function as intertexts to the scriptural canon, and how far was pseudepigraphy playful or even casual? To give an obvious example: the Mishnah is ostensibly a pseudepigraphon: the 'oral law' given to Moses on Sinai. Yet it is full of the sayings of Tannaitic (pre-second century CE) rabbis. That Moses would not have understood his own torah as expounded by the famous Rabbi Akiva is one of the well-known jokes of rabbinic literature. Here, clearly, pseudepigraphy is not deceptive, either in intent or effect.

But the case of the Mishnah is perhaps exceptional, or at least suggests that there is no single motivation for ancient Jewish and Christian pseudepigraphy. We can say, though, that the sudden emergence of so many writings of long-dead persons, far from arousing suspicion, was accepted, at least by the *literati*, constituting one of the more fashionable genres of the day. Part of the reason for this fashion may well have been the impact of a Greek-Hellenistic tradition of *named* authors on a largely *anonymous* tradition of composition in the cultures of the Fertile Crescent. Perhaps pseudepigraphy itself is another symptom of that fusion of Greek and Oriental traditions that we call 'Hellenism'.[1]

Character and Biblical Narrative
What is equally interesting, however, is that such Jewish works only rarely exploited the *character* of the individual concerned. Occasionally the symbolic role of the eponymous author played some part (as with a Levi or a Judah representing priesthood and kingship, or an Ezra the torah), but the content of the pseudepigraphon was rarely concerned to fill in gaps concerning the life of the 'author' (as distinct from non-autobiographical genres, such as the *Prayer of Manasseh* or the *Martyrdom of Isaiah*; the Qumran *Genesis Apocryphon* being a partial exception, apparently narrated in the name of Lamech). The pseudo-authors were generally required to know, or to learn, of the future, and it mattered not very often, or not very much, whether they be Abraham or Jacob, Solomon or Isaiah. A venerable name was mostly what mattered, and a knowledge of their biblical life was not usually a prerequisite. So pseudepigraphy was not essentially a mode of hagiography (a genre that certainly existed), nor was it as a rule a mode of biblical interpretation, an exegetical genre.

These observations make it clear that the modern pseudepigraphy in this volume is quite different, for the implied reader is expected to have a decent knowledge of, and interest in, the biblical *character*, and expects her or him to be amplified. The private lives of the famous, whether real or fictional (is there a difference?) are part of our cultural diet. But such a learned or semi-learned exercise in the world of early Judaism generally took a non-autobiographical form. Biblical stories certainly *could* be retold, and were often quite markedly altered in the process. Thus, for example, Isaiah became a martyr, while Isaac and Jephthah's daughter were made into active participants in their own offering. The profile of ancient characters could also, with or without an explicit narrative, undergo drastic revision: Balaam, for instance, moved from near-hero to villain (see the excellent treatment in Vermes 1973), while Tamar and Rahab were also surprisingly well-remembered, included among other things as ancestors of Jesus in the gospel of Matthew. The case of the Adam literature is probably different: this probably did not seek to rescue

1. Why does the author of Qoheleth use a pseudepigraph while ben Sira—or rather his grandson—does not? In this respect ben Sira is more 'Greek'!

him from a poor reputation but preserved an older tradition about his glorious status. Biblical characters were available for redefinition, embellishment and re-evaluation by early Jewish writers, but not in the pseudepigraphic genre. (And it could be argued that in none of the Jewish genres do we find much interest in character development: character is effaced by type.)

The modern interest in *character* represents a marked difference from ancient Jewish pseudepigraphy. Indeed, the narrative of the Hebrew Bible is in no way interested in exploring character as such: as locus of conflicting emotion, duty or rationality, as an engine of plot. Internal tension has to be inferred (and modern literary criticism can do this *ad infinitum*), but it is remains to be demonstrated that the psychological profile of any biblical character is deeply explored, where explored at all. By contrast, the Greek dramatists exploited to a great extent the notion of the tragic individual caught in a web of conflicting forces that could only end in that character's destruction. Without a single god to impose moral order, the heroes of Aeschylus, Sophocles and Euripides were humans left to cope with the whims of various gods, with the duties imposed by society, and with the internal compulsions of loyalty, the conflicts between which drive them to their fate. To this focus we moderns respond more readily, I think. The notion of the individual is, I would suggest, not a Judaeo-Christian, but a Graeco-Roman one.

Modern Pseudepigraphy

The biblical characters speaking in this book of modern pseudepigraphy talk above all directly from such an inner life: about feelings, intentions, hopes, regrets—dimensions of personality virtually absent in the Hebrew Bible. There is, however, one interesting feature they share with ancient pseudepigraphic authors: foreknowledge. Many of the pseudo-authors in this book know of, and talk about, their own future, their fate at the hands of centuries of reception, as players in the canonical drama. They are destined to suffer the fate of fame, the price of which (as with all fame) is to lose control of one's identity, to surrender it to others, to become an icon. Many of the characters in this book will protest that they are not these icons, that they have been betrayed. Modern biblical pseudepigraphy is an engagement with the history of reception, which is typically played off against the biblical text.

Of course, this is a device familiar to narratologists: readers fill in gaps when reading stories and the leaving of gaps by the author of any narrative is both inevitable and productive (Iser 1978). Yet what is especially remarkable about this exercise in the case of Hebrew biblical characters is *the size of the gaps and the consequent ease with which characters can be reconstructed in quite different ways*. Because character is, as I observed earlier, much less a focus of biblical than of modern narrative, much less exploited as an engine of events (at least explicitly), the reader is afforded a great deal of freedom in reading characters. Biblical narratives offer a large scope for retelling. The story may be strong, but the *fabula* (the narrated sequence, setting and cast of characters) may be cast in any number of different stories, let alone different texts.

In the case of biblical narrative, and especially in this volume, the distinction between *fabula* and story is exploited. In effect, and mainly by retelling character, a *fabula* implied by a biblical story can be reconstituted in a new story. There is a parallel in historical reconstruction: there, scholars are quite used to the notion that a historical event (such as the siege of Jerusalem by Sennacherib—not a perfect example) is capable of being told by different sources so as to generate different testimonies, without the sources necessarily distorting events. In a non-historical mode of exegesis, the *fabula* has no correspondence in a historical world, but it has some degree of objectivity in relation to a story by means of which it is narrated. An event may be narrated accurately enough in the form of several differing accounts, and similarly a *fabula* can be represented accurately in several stories. Modern scholarly autobiography, like historical fiction, does not work if it departs too much from the received *fabula*, which ought to remain more or less intact. This is how Yairah Amit, rather differently, puts the issue in her essay:

> it is a primary rule that an artistic work based on a character drawn from a familiar textual tradition, if it seeks to retain its link with the original work in order to give the new one added depth, must show some loyalty to the tradition on which it rests. The link enables the reader, or viewer, to recall the original, so that it may serve as a basis for comparison and for the appreciation of the singular new work (p. 69).

But since, as mentioned earlier, biblical characters are so easily re-storied because of their lack of strong internal profile, why, until fairly recently, have they been so little re-read in literary media (Thomas Mann's Joseph and the Davids of Stefan Heim and Joseph Heller being the great modern exercises in this rereading)? Perhaps the freedom that biblical Hebrew narrative affords has been more than compensated for by the weight of a tradition (comprising sacred stories) that has to a very great extent canonized even the profiles of characters (see Barbour 1987). To return to the analogy with history: the 'biblical theology' movement tried to relocate the substance of the testimony of the Hebrew Bible away from the narrative towards the event, a tendency that has been since reversed. But in literary studies the distinction between the biblical story and the *fabula* remains blurred, and we talk rather about retelling or deconstructing or interpreting the biblical *story*, when we are often either rereading the *text* or retelling the *fabula*.

Dramatis personae

What sort of stories is this volume telling? Some authors seek to redraw the biblical characters and their predicaments into the modern life of the Christian by, for instance, taking Gomer and Hosea to the marriage counsellor. Others' stories will maintain a different distance, standing far from the history of (religious) reception. For different constituencies, the exercise is liberating, both for the *fabula* and for the reader. However, the reader can probably be expected to embrace joyfully some contributions and grimace at others.

The following autobiographies (not all are strictly autobiographies, but all are 'first person') feature characters for whom the authors feel there is a need to speak, those with a grievance, or suffering a malady of chronic misprision. Many of us are probably writing in an obliquely *genuine* autobiographical mode, identifying in some way with the characters chosen, using them as our voice, much as the prophets use Yahweh as theirs. Those readers who are not personally familiar with any author are free to (mis-)construct us accordingly (see Moore 1995).

In commissioning this volume, I did not instruct the authors whose voice to take or how to speak. I conceived the volume as an experiment, to some degree, in how a biblical scholar might exploit the genre. There are clearly many possibilities. What is noteworthy, though on reflection not entirely surprising, is that on the whole minor characters have been selected to speak: women, non-Israelite. This is not only, I suspect, because minor characters in the Bible offer more scope for creative exegesis (since I don't think this is actually true!), but because of a desire to retrieve the marginalized voice, a technique now endemic in modern biblical interpretation. Whatever, the choice is somehow significant.

In the opening contribution by Suzanne Shaw, we find not a single autobiography, but a range of characters and multiple viewpoints reflecting on a single episode, the story of Judah and Tamar (or Tamar and Judah) in Genesis 38. The voices of characters in the narrative and in the surrounding Joseph narrative enable her to exploit the many problems of the story itself, including the ethics of Tamar's and Judah's behaviour and the relationship of the story to the Joseph narrative in general. But by including characters from elsewhere in the Bible, she can also deal with issues of intertextuality and canonical context. The approach thus delivers a large number of relevant exegetical and interpretative perspectives. But in order to do so, it inevitably stretches some fictional boundaries. As Shaw says,

> I have imbued the authors with a much broader perspective than would have been possible or realistic for them, a perspective that includes the hindsight of several millennia of history, the coming of Christ, and a fair amount of comment from biblical scholars (p. 25).

The perspective of modern scholarship is intrinsic to the genre of modern pseudepigraphy being exemplified here. The explicitly Christian perspective is another matter. Implying that characters in the Old Testament would reflect on their past from the perspective of the New Testament, baptizing them, as it were, constitutes a particular claim: about the extent of the canon, and of the fulfilment of Judaism in Christianity. But this is what the New Testament itself does, while ancient Jewish texts like the book of *Jubilees* impose the Mosaic law upon the pre-Sinai ancestors. Would the biblical story allow any of Abraham's ancestors to embrace Christianity? The Jewish and non-religious pseudo-autobiographers here will certainly not follow this lead. But Shaw's is not the only explicitly Christian reading in this book, and all take advantage of hindsight.

Shaw's 'letters' are not to God but to the author of Genesis, and this very human compiler, if acknowledged to have been making the best effort to convey the truth about the Jewish (and Christian) god, is not beyond criticism for the strong gender bias that his book exhibits. There is, after all, hardly any kind of feminism that will try (let alone succeed) totally to 'redeem' the biblical text, surely? And Shaw does not want to involve a single male God who is claimed as the author of patriarchal laws, in her criticism. She actually opposes patriarchalism in the name of God (and in the voice of Rachel):

> Gentlewomen, it's clear that we've all been victims of this editorial process called life. We've been left out and written out, disappeared, died, and been overshadowed (and not by the Holy Spirit!) Only a few of our stories have been told, and even then only in part, and only from the point of view of the

men to whom we related or the men to whom the story was relayed. The whole of the people of Israel, and I dare say the whole world, has suffered and suffers still from the permanent lack and loss of our distinctive voices. Something essential about the character of God and the image of God has been tragically lost. For our own sake and for the sake of humanity, no longer should we allow what men say about us to be the final word! (p. 43).

And 'what men say' is, after all 'what the Bible says'. Letters to the editor of Genesis are perhaps letters of feminism to…men? Her Eve says:

Men have wronged us and we are victims personally and corporately of abuses of power. But we have been passive accomplices of our own silence. It's time to speak out, and I thank the editor [of Genesis] for doing his part in allowing our voices to be heard now (p. 45).

The editor of Genesis (who has the last word!), for his part pleads that 'in entrusting me and all of us to the process [of writing down], he allowed room for discrepancy at best, and error and selfish propaganda at worst. I shall have to account for the writing and editing job that I do…' (p. 46).

Shaw's biblical theology leaves the Bible as a very fallible male human record for which God (and we?) will call the authors to account. (Would such a theology also extend to the New Testament?) Perhaps Shaw is too kind to her biblical author and her God. Some men, and even women, however, may think it too unkind to them. Either way, this is quite a thought-provoking essay.

Athalya Brenner, who is both Israeli and feminist, opts for the voice of a woman, Raḥab, who is not Israelite, not Jewish, and has acquired a contradictory reputation as a harlot and a traitor, a convert and even a matriarch. The story is annotated by a rich selection of Jewish (and some Christian) interpretations of Raḥab, but also confronts deeper material and philosophical issues. On the material side we hear of the precariousness of urban life on the fringes of the desert; of the rates of infant mortality; of the techniques of abortion and contraception known to Raḥab in her profession as the 'madam of Jericho'. A story about the negotiation between settled Canaanites and invading Israelites also allows her to reflect on the strong ties between peoples and territories: her 'beloved Jericho' has been occupied by Jews, Arabs, Canaanites, Israelites…and it continues to exist as the place of Raḥab's affections. And history gives way to philosophy, or rather leads into it: 'My beloved city will return, only to be reconquered and retaken, demolished and rebuilt, inhabited and deserted' (p. 58). So Raḥab continues to 'observe it, and observe history and the way it is constructed' (p. 57).

And Raḥab herself, 'the Broad' is of course also constructed:

> ...I have the feeling that they have constructed me as an anonymous woman,
> a nicknamed whore, in order to emphasize my faith or whatever else they
> attribute to me... If a whore has faith, anybody else should (pp. 56-57).

In Raḥab's eternal voice one hears the time of *longue durée*, of a history transcending the short and violent span of the biblical narratives, a history of women's experience, of the constant rewriting of history into myth and legend, the shaping of personality into icon or stereotype; of the endless human cycle of betrayal, conquest, defeat, life and death played on an eternal stage. This is the lesson not of Raḥab's *Leben*, but of her *Nachleben*.

At first it seems that Yairah Amit, also Israeli, has chosen, like Athalya Brenner, to assume the voice of a non-Israelite, Delilah. But quite the reverse. She argues that while many modern commentators make Delilah a Philistine, sometimes for obvious reasons, the early Jewish sages had it differently, and correctly:

> Some of them understood a woman's suffering, and they regarded me as a
> flesh-and-blood woman with desires and needs of her own, not a woman to
> be condemned, but Samson's wife, who was not a too-devoted spouse but
> was neither a Philistine nor a harlot (p. 64).

So who is the villain responsible for her change of identity? (Read and see!)

The first part of Amit's 'autobiography' is in fact about readings and the history of reading and misreading of Delilah, with an especially useful survey of her appearance in European fine art. It also underlines the truth that to become an immortal character means to suffer the prejudices of 'tradition', to become a stereotype, or even more than one stereotype:

> I feel flattered by this variety of approaches, delighted to have stirred the
> imagination of so many artists, but on the other hand, I am often angered by
> their one-sidedness, their obsession with the scene in which Samson's eyes
> are put out, and when they adapt me to fit Christian contexts, which are not
> really to my taste. But one cannot have everything, and this is the price I
> must pay for my bit of eternity in the museums and galleries that contain
> the best of Western civilization (p. 69).

The truth is, of course, that fictional characters have no stable essence: they are born as inventions of an artist and they will remain the creations and recreations of other artists. What else however, can one do with literary creations? (Only make the error of turning them into historical characters!)

Hugh Pyper's Jezebel has fared even worse than Delilah at the hands of the biblical narrator, and no less in subsequent history where her name has become a byword. Even so, her dignity in the face of death has nearly always impressed the sensitive reader, and in her own story that pride is given full justification. But while in the books of Kings she is the target of a hate that is religiously motivated, here she is shown as no less devout to her divine mistress than were Elijah or Elisha to their master, and we are invited to imagine the piety of a goddess religion, even if at the behest of a 'man, of sorts, sitting in a book-lined room, unanswered letters and student papers on his desk, tapping away at a keyboard, rearranging electrons on a screen' (p. 78). And whose people, she asks, gave our world its alphabet?

But most strikingly of all, Pyper's Jezebel is challenging:

> But you, you who read this—what are you looking at when you look at me? Is it not the goddess, the mother, the wicked witch who thwarts, cajoles and ultimately betrays you, who you see die in me? Do I not carry every woman's burden where men allay their fears through wrecking women's bodies?...What peace are you seeking? What peace do I disturb in you? (pp. 91-92).

and not only defiant but victorious:

> [I]s not the goddess, who can never die, returning to her own at last, showing weak and vicious men that all their violence and bluster can never change the fact that it is in the womb of women that the world is formed? (p. 92).

Francis Landy's recent engagement with the book of Isaiah continues as he explores the mystery of the prophetic voice, as both universal divine voice and as a dimension of prophetic psychology. Like some others in this volume, Landy takes seriously the religious dimension of the book, the text and a highly religious, undoubtedly Jewish, but in many respects also universally human perspective. Here is no fissure between text and reception: the voice of Isaiah transcends time even though its utterance is historically situated. Landy's Isaiah is a man, born into a real world; but this man sees himself, feels himself, as a voice; and it is of course as a voice that we read him. But the voice is also the voice of God.

> A voice says, 'Cry out!' And I said, 'What shall I cry?' All flesh is grass, and all its integrity like a wild flower... The grass withers, the flower fades: but the word of our God will stand for ever... (Isa. 40.6, 8).

Isaiah as voice is written by Isaiah ben Amoz, whose mother is Zion and whose father is God. His voice is also the voice of Moses, the voice of Jonah, the voice that rests everywhere, belongs nowhere:

> I am, incarnation and cohabitation with so many bodies, this voice, never
> quite at home, that comes and speaks in the womb, come, be, belong, be
> filled with light and immensity, this immense labour, forming the words,
> the book, leaving it unsettled, to work its strange work, in you, who are also
> I, in whom I cohabit, sometimes, this book, this strange book, to which I
> belong, which is me, so unfinished, so unsettled: we, once, before the word,
> the voice, we once…were (p. 93).

It is also a voice that comes out of, and disappears into, silence. But it is
made flesh, and we read of its incarnation: Landy's Isaiah depicts his early
life with vivid images of voyages and lands beyond Judah before returning
to the world of an apprentice prophet in Jerusalem, meeting with his
teacher and fellow apprentices every sabbath to discuss torah, the voice of
God—the voice that they expected would inhabit them too. But Isaiah
remains a man of the world, a lover of women and children, in love with a
world full of signs, whose gaze meets knowingly with the lion's, whose
body vibrates to all the sounds of the world.

But the divine voice comes, shatters and transforms this person's life.
He sees the Face, beholds the light and then becomes a prophet, the Voice.
He parts from the world. But to write the silent voice into poetry: that is
hard and the labour is described with great intensity. Hearing is one thing,
speaking another, and pervading his speech, all speech, is silence and
death, knowledge of extinction and desire for it. Isaiah the man is haunted,
just as his voice haunts. Or so I read this Isaiah, reading also Francis
Landy, a writer like no other.

Hosea has had his say for millennia, and in recent years Gomer has
found her own voice (see, e.g., Sherwood 1996). For many feminist (and
other) readers, the prophet is a wife-abuser. His victim speaks twice in this
book. Jonathan Magonet's Gomer, without doubt the wittiest writer in the
entire volume, and President of Adulteresses Anonymous (AA), is a
member of the Women Against Patriarchy Consciousness Raising Committee, whose meetings necessarily take place in secret but whose
members find themselves no less uneasy in her presence than would a
male gathering. Gomer is a double outsider. But she speaks to the
assembled women, who include Sarah, Ruth, Huldah and the anonymous
sisters of Zelophehad of her motives. The problem is not only the abusive
husband, but his recent conviction that he is a prophet and must write. This
means big trouble: the book will be worse than the man:

> Hosea has God, the priests, the guild of prophets and half the men in the
> country on his side, and this time he's added violence to the mixture. So
> we've got to do something to stop him. A prophetic scroll like this could be

> all the excuse they need to lock us up, beat us, and maybe one day even
> burn us at the stake, all in the name of God (p. 118).

She stops speaking, and realizes that in this time and place such things could not be heard. And that she is already pregnant. Her story is about to begin, and it is too late. Beneath the light touch lurks the rhetorical question: would it have been better if the book of Hosea had never been written? The real question, of course is: what can we, whether men or women, do with it? The lightness of touch in this piece is deceptive: the issues he raises are as deep and as clearly exposed as any in this volume.

Gillian Cooper and John Goldingay have exploited their joint-gendered-authorship to explore the two-sidedness of the Hosea–Gomer relationship, and to use this as a basis for the practical exploration of modern relationships. They introduce their essay with presentation of their own position: 'It would be inappropriate', they say, 'to ricochet from a demonizing of Gomer to a demonizing of Hosea' (p. 119). Thus, they will allow both Hosea and Gomer to speak to the marriage counsellor, reconciliation being the aim, exegetically as well as maritally. At all events, like Shaw's essay, this works with the text rather than against it, expressing a hermeneutic that is committed to the value of the text without being at all uncritical of its problems. For in such situations the husband's and wife's stories are each plausible, reasonable, coherent and yet incompatible, which provides an apt metaphor for biblical interpretation itself.

What makes this essay especially compelling is that Cooper and Goldingay, having each taken the respective gender roles and drafted their account, role-played their biblical characters with a marriage counsellor and in the light of that rewrote their parts for this essay, and they invite readers to read aloud the pleas on both sides, thus adopting the personae themselves. And indeed, why should the reader remain passive rather than participate in the exercise of biblical autobiography?

In a famous interview, Princess Diana complained that her marriage to Prince Charles was 'crowded; it felt as if there were three people'; Gomer makes the same complaint here, but referring to Yahweh:

> He was always first for me, no matter who my other friends were—and
> some of them were more lovers than friends, I admit it. I've never been first
> for him, though. Another woman—I could have dealt with that, you can
> fight another woman, you are on common ground then. But you can't
> compete with God (p. 127).

For his part, Hosea found his marriage even more crowded:

> She always said that none of those other young men meant anything to her. She said she loved me for the solidness and security and strength that I represented. But I never could understand why she wanted to spend all that time with them if they meant nothing to her. I used to imagine what they got up to. I challenged her about it. I said I knew she had affairs with them. I wasn't even sure that Uncared-for and Unpeopled were actually mine. I said I wanted to know what happened between her and those other men, but she refused to tell me. She wanted her own life as well as a life with me, she said. She didn't want to have to tell me everything about every relationship. I couldn't cope with that. I wanted to tell her everything about me (not that there was much to tell). I wanted us to be one, not separate people. As long as she wouldn't tell me, I could only suppose what went on (p. 126).

'Why is my being committed to Yahweh a problem?' says Hosea in his first response. Cooper and Goldingay are not, of course dealing with an historical relationship but one that is symbolic. By recycling this symbolic relationship as a (not untypical) modern one, they are constructing a Christian theology of marriage too. But perhaps a not too conventional one. Still, I would think that for Goldingay and Cooper all marriages have a third person.

Finally, the essay by Davies treads, characteristically, upon a delicate issue, genocide and racist hatred, and, as he has previously attempted with Abraham (Davies 1995), he seeks to undermine one of the strongest readings in the history of biblical interpretation by reversing (I think he might even prefer me to say 'correcting') the roles of hero and villain in the story of Esther. Here, as with several of the other contributions, the text lends its support with surprising readiness, confirming that there is no record of Agagite (i.e. Amalekite) hatred of Israel, but rather the reverse. So often in literature and history, the Jew is the outsider: here is the Jews' own favourite outsider turned victim, turned author.

The history of exegesis of Esther has, indeed, been generally distracted from the issue of Mordecai's motivation which, arguably, is the key to the book's plot rather than Haman's supposed hatred of Jews. Understandably, huge efforts have been expended in diminishing or explaining away the joy of extermination on the part of the Jews: thus, the book of Esther is seen as parodic, or as fantasy literature, or as comic. But the exercise is rather one-sided: why go to lengths to excuse Jewish genocide but take for granted the genocidal psyche of Haman?

For Davies, Haman is indeed the victim and one whose crime has been very ironically compounded by centuries of persecution of Jews for which this fictional character stands as the canonical symbol. But when the grain is racial hatred, what scriptural book more urgently needs to be 'read against'?

I wish the reader of this book much joy, expect some dismay, and issue an invitation to 'go and do likewise'. For I think it is by far the most rewarding, potentially subtle and readable form of biblical scholarship I have yet engaged in, whether as author, editor or reader.

LETTERS TO THE EDITOR OF GENESIS

Suzanne Shaw

What follows is a set of letters written to the editor of Genesis, a book which began as a serial in a weekly newsletter or magazine in circulation among the Israelite people. In the lively correspondence section of this magazine, readers, including the central characters of the stories, were invited to write in with questions, opinions, additional details and perspectives, confrontations and challenges to these articles. The collection concludes with a response from the magazine's editor before he compiled these stories into the collection now in the Bible. From the selection of letters I have made, the central focus is on the story that became ch. 38 in Genesis, the curious but obviously provocative story of Judah and Tamar (which some readers thought had been inserted by mistake into the Joseph story, but which apparently was indeed in the right place).

The fictional nature of these exchanges is rather underscored because their assigned authors know more than they would have known in the context of their lifetime. For example, several of the characters mention Jesus, or New Testament scripture, or modern-day idiomatic expressions. I have imbued the authors with a much broader perspective than would have been possible or realistic for them, a perspective that includes the hindsight of several millennia of history, the coming of Christ, and a fair amount of comment from biblical scholars. On the other hand, however, I limit (or possibly eliminate) the characters' fully ancient Hebrew perspectives with the imposition of my own context of being a white, middle-class educated Protestant American woman psychologist at the beginning of the twenty-first century. I wish I could read the real letters these people would have written!

Table of Contents

Letter 1: From Joseph

I have heard the buzz all the way to Egypt about how people are upset that you interrupted the great story you were doing on my life with this seemingly unconnected, irrelevant piece on my brother and his daughter-in-law.[1] What do Judah and Tamar have to do with anything?, they ask.[2] Well, I am flattered by the support of the devoted readership. However, not only in defense of your editing choice but in defense of myself as well, I think the addition of ch. 38 between my being sold to Egypt and the juicy

---

1.   Many commentators—ancient, medieval and contemporary—have arrived at this conclusion. Wright (1982: 523) cites five; Goldin (1977: 27) notes three more; Alter (1981: 3) and Mathewson (1989: 373 n. 5) cite one more each. Brueggemann (1982: 307) even denounces ch. 38 as isolated, enigmatic, not belonging, and not theologically significant, although in my opinion he goes on to make some significant theological observations from it, regarding a redefinition of righteousness in terms of community.

2.   Even commentators who agree that ch. 38 is well placed disagree on its main purpose or its relevance to Genesis as a whole. The tracing of (Jewish) tribal history/ genealogy are commonly proposed theories (Mathewson 1989: 388 n. 73; Brueggemann 1982: 308; Rendsburg 1986: 441). Along these lines, Menn proposes its main thrust is the transition to the next generation, while Rendsburg (1986: 441) asserts it is to 'adumbrate events from the life of Israel's greatest king (David)'; Brueggemann proposes that a radical moral critique and understanding of righteousness propels the passage (Brueggemann 1982: 311). Goldin cites three rabbinic theories about the chapter as the connecting link on themes of descent, recognition and Tamar/Potiphar's wife (Goldin 1977: 28-29). According to Mathewson (1989: 389 n. 83), citing Ross, it contributes to Genesis's overall theme of the 'sovereignty of Yahweh in His establishment of a nation through which to bless all the peoples of the world'. He elaborates: the purposes of God are at work in hidden but reliable ways which will come to fruition. Ironically, this is Brueggemann's thesis for Gen. 37–50, but he fails to apply it to ch. 38. However, Plaut does so specifically (Mathewson 1989: 390).

details of Potiphar's wife's attempted seduction of me is a well-placed work of literary genius.[3] I must say, although I am neither vengeful nor vindictive towards my brother Judah, I do appreciate the irony of his situation.[4] Wouldn't you agree with me that the *lex talionis* might be paraphrased, 'An injustice for an injustice?'[5] As I myself went down to Egypt (those 'vicious rumors' you heard about my jealous brothers' evil plot to get rid of me were indeed true), my poor grief-wracked father vowed to *go down* to Sheol because of his sorrow over me, the favorite son of his favorite wife. Well, now you see that Judah too *went down* both literally and figuratively.[6]

The placement of ch. 38 after 37 highlights the contrast between my father's deep attachment and love for me (that he 'refused to be comforted', so I hear)[7] and my brother's apparently little remorse for either of his sons,[8] and his pursuit of fleeting pleasures quickly after having 'been comforted' of the loss of his wife.[9] So I must say, although I feel bad for the embarrassment my brother surely suffered, there was a poetic justice about it all and it certainly reflects well on me, don't you think? Judah always thought I was a silly 'dreamer'. Well, I guess it's true when they say a prophet is never welcome in his own land. But hey, time and the Holy One, Blessed be He, seem to have a way of working these things out in the strangest ways! We all know the ending to this story: I did rule over my brothers and saved my family's—and thus all of Israel's—lives. In a way, Judah's story—far from being merely a 'meanwhile' sideline—actually heightens the excitement and tension of my own story: what was happening to me in this foreign land during the

---

3.   Alter 1996: 217. Mathewson cites Benno Jacob's assessment of ch. 38 as the 'crown of the book of Genesis' (Mathewson 1989: 373). Rather than having a theory of a sole purpose, why couldn't all of the above theories (see n. 2) be true to some degree? The mastery of Gen. 38 is that it parallels and echoes pieces from the chapters immediately before and after it (Cassuto argues that intertextual parallels between chs. 37 and 38 provide 'a kind of internal nexus'[Mathewson 1989: 386]), from Genesis as a whole and other biblical books, while remaining a story which stands on its own.

4.   Menn (1997: 35-41) details at length the irony of Judah's character and situation.

5.   Menn (1997: 315) cites the *Midrash Haggadol* explanation that Judah's 'going down' was caused by his sale of Joseph.

6.   Alter 1981: 4, 6; Menn 1997: 37-38.

7.   Alter 1981: 4 and 11, citing *Ber. R.* 84.11, 12.

8.   Alter 1981: 10; 1996: 220.

9.   Alter 1981: 7; 1996: 220; Frankel 1996: 76-77; Gunn and Fewell 1993: 37-38.

22 years that lapsed between my disappearance and rediscovery?[10] I send my kudos for a brilliant editing job; please don't move ch. 38 back or forward, as some have so forcefully argued you should do.[11]

Letter 2: From Judah

In response to Joseph's letter of the other week: A bit of sibling rivalry still, eh? I guess he comes by it honestly; it seems to run in the family. I guess that's what happens when there are 12 of us plus sisters and wives all jostling for dear old daddy's attention and favor! At the risk of seeming insecure, I take umbrage at Joseph's claim to Gen. 37–50 as 'his story'! That's a bit egocentric, don't you think? But then, Joseph has always felt that feeling of 'specialness' (mild delusions of grandeur?) that sets him apart. I am willing to set my life in the context of our father Jacob's story,[12] and in a larger context of the story of the people of God, and ultimately the story of God himself. But I am not willing to concede that my life is set in the context of my younger brother's (sorry, bro!).[13] As sons of Israel, my other brothers (Reuben, Simeon and Levi in particular) and I believe that we, too, have stories to tell in our own right. Yes, I do admit that I have endured some public humiliation which has been called my 'descent'. But let's look at the rest of the story! All's well that ends

10. Wright 1982: 523 n. 3.

11. The book of *Jubilees* moves ch. 38 to ch. 41 of Genesis (Goldin 1977: 27). Mathewson asserts that 'despite chronological difficulties, any other placement would cause even more difficulty' (Mathewson 1989: 381; 382 n. 47). Even Speiser, who sees the chapter as disconnected, admits the placement was 'chosen with keen literary sensitivity' (Speiser 1964: 384). Historian Josephus omitted it entirely from the Joseph story in his *Antiquities of the Jews* (Speiser 1964: 374), as did Elliott (1961). Now that's one way to get rid of a difficult passage! Unfortunately they have missed the richness inherent in its complexity and ambiguity.

12. Mathewson (1989: 385) recalls that 'while Genesis 37–50 is often identified as the Joseph story', Gen. 37.2 opens and identifies that section as 'the generations of Jacob'.

13. Goldin (1977: 28) proposes that ch. 38 adds yet another example to one of the 'major themes of Genesis, and beyond—the triumph of the younger son over the older'. Recall Cain and Abel, Isaac and Ishmael, Jacob and Esau, Ephraim and Manasseh; he also points out that Shem, Abraham, Moses, Gideon, Jotham and David were probably youngest sons (at least, certainly not the eldest). His emphasis on the younger-son theme is that God subverts the 'law' of the firstborn and establishes his right to choose patriarchs as he pleases. Also, in narrative form, the stories are an outlet for subtle rebellion and resentment of non-firstborns while maintaining order (Goldin 1977: 44).

well. For the two sons I lost I got two more. My name has not only been cleared of shame but has become the very name by which our people, the Jews, are called. Joseph did rule over me temporarily, but in the long run the descendants of my tribe are the kings and rulers over all of Israel by our own father's decree! I have even been called Genesis 38's counterpart to King David.[14] I need not even mention (though I will because I think it further proves my point) that through my son Perez came the ultimate Ruler, Jesus. Isn't this surely enough evidence of Yhwh's divine mercy: forgiveness, restitution, redemption and blessing?

Yes, Joseph was our father's favorite, I agree. I see now I was foolish to try to undo that. Just because Joseph was the favorite didn't mean the rest of us weren't owed our due. We all know the common law that the firstborn-son receives a double portion of the inheritance,[15] even if he is of the less-loved wife (Deut. 21.15-17). But Reuben, whom we all know is the naturally expected recipient of the firstborn-son privileges, acted arrogantly and presumptuously in taking Dad's concubine Bilhah for himself, as if he had already assumed rulership of the clan.[16] Dad kept quiet at the time, but we could all tell he was humiliated and fuming inside. Anyway, Reuben's premature claim actually cost him his blessing and excluded him from the 'race'. Then Simeon and Levi dishonored our father and put themselves out of the running when they violently and somewhat irreverently decimated the Shechemites (some might complain that they flippantly or profanely applied the sign of the covenant for the enemies' demise). Sure, our sister Dinah was appreciative of the irony of the strategy employing their tender genitals as their weakness, and also grateful for fierce brotherly loyalty to avenge the violation of her honor[17]

14. Rendsburg gives an argument for the intertextuality between Gen. 38 and 1 and 2 Sam., with priority on the Davidic narrative, finding parallels in the cast of characters (see his chart of correspondences where Judah = David (Rendsburg 1986: 441). Why? He asserts that it is (Gen. 38) author's intent to 'poke fun at the royal family', the purpose being for entertainment. Apparently Judah has missed the subtlety and mockery of such a 'compliment'!

15. Goldin 1977: 29.

16. Goldin 1977: 37. The incident referred to occurs in Gen. 35.22.

17. It is interesting that the two older brothers who did not retaliate against Dinah's offenders, Judah and Reuben, are the same ones guilty of sexually questionable behaviors. Reuben slept with his father's concubine. Gunn and Fewell (1993: 35) observe that the same set of verbs—see, take and lie with—are used in both Dinah's rape and Judah's relationship to his wife Batshua. Judah also has no qualms about relations with a harlot, which is the word Simeon and Levi use to describe the way

(about which Dad was strangely silent). That brought the story necessarily to me, the fourth-born, as the rightful recipient of the double portion[18]... and doesn't the blessing of my twin sons top it off nicely?[19] ['Grandpa' Jacob was just tickled pink about his little usurping grandson, Perez, overcoming his red-stringed brother. Uncle 'Red' Esau didn't find it quite so humorous; he just *tsk-tsk*'d and shook his head.] Hey, Joseph himself said it, and on this point I do agree: God works in mysterious ways. I was not beyond redemption.[20] Let's give credit where credit is due; after seeing the error of my ways, I really matured and took more responsibility and leadership.[21] That was a turning point for me, and the way was up, up, up from there.[22]

Letter 3: From Tamar

Since when has the editorial page been a forum for sibling rivalry? I can't even believe that these two brothers are at it again about power and status and who is greater than whom![23] I mean, have we forgotten that the story

---

their sister had been treated (Gen. 34.31). Could it be that Reuben and Simeon's sexual morals or consciences were somehow diminished so as not to feel what was done to their sister was so grave a crime? Or perhaps Simeon and Levi's weakness was not sexuality but violent anger.

18. Goldin 1997: 42-43 suggests that the insertion of ch. 38 is to inform the reader about Judah's life, the 'vita of the chosen one'.

19. From Judah's point-of-view, this final scene corrects an imbalance caused by the loss of two of his original sons (Gunn and Fewell 1993: 44). Ironically, he seems to see neither God's responsibility in his loss nor his own responsibility in causing the loss of a son (Joseph) to his father. Maddox (1987: 15) claims the twin sons as a double blessing for Tamar rather than Judah.

20. There are several ways of seeing redemption in the Tamar–Judah story. Frankel (1996: 79) says Judah himself redeemed his primary pledge through owning up to what he'd done. It is not clear whether this 'primary pledge' of which she speaks is the levirate obligation to provide a father for Tamar's descendants, or his staff, ring and cord. Conversely, Tamar redeemed Judah's heirlessness. Because there is no apparent condemnation of Judah from God's point of view in the narrative, as there was on Er and Onan, there is no apparent need for redemption, either. Mathewson (1989: 390) says that Yahweh accomplished his purposes despite Judah's unfaithfulness.

21. Menn 1997: 43.

22. Mathewson (1989: 375-76) has called the Judah–Tamar story a comedy because of its 'U-shaped' plot (tragic circumstances turned to happy ending through a reversal of fortune is the basic form).

23. 'If one reads this episode as part of the patriarchal story, one can hardly miss the common motif of brothers struggling for status. Beginning with the competition

we're discussing here is not only about Judah but about me, too? What is all this to-do about Judah's rise to greatness? What about me and my sons; why were we dropped like a hot potato? So many people (even people I have never heard of) have written me supportive letters admiring what I did, even supporting it, in light of my awful circumstances. I mean, it boggles my mind how this story has gotten around with me as the supposed 'heroine' and yet I'm barely a person in it![24] For example, Judah refers to me as his 'daughter-in-law' (self-indictingly so, as he failed to fulfill the implied commitment and responsibility of that relationship on his end),[25] and I am variously referred to as 'a wife for Er', 'your/my brother's wife' (by Judah and Onan), 'a widow', 'the woman' and 'the harlot'. Do I not have rights and an identity of my own, or only in relation to the men in my life?[26] I tell myself I shouldn't really be complaining; Judah's wife didn't even get the dignity of her name mentioned once, known only as Batshua, or the daughter of Shua. Still, I find it darkly paradoxical that I had to be mistaken for someone else in order to get that which was rightly mine and which I depended on, namely my children. I guess I risked my 'descent' too, into compromised womanhood and sub-personhood, in order to emerge on the other side as more fully woman and more fully human as a mother and as a belonging—not central, but at least not marginal—member of my community.[27] Still, in the end of my whole ordeal, for which I endangered my life (and nearly lost it!), I remain husbandless.

My emerging sons, and even my midwife, eclipse me as I am abruptly relegated to the status of a womb![28] That is, I didn't get the credit for the

between Cain and Abel, we have watched parental favoritism and the custom of primogeniture create strife between siblings as they struggle for birthright, blessing, inheritance, power' (Gunn and Fewell 1993: 44).

24. Menn (1997: 28-29) calls Tamar the 'marginal protagonist' and describes the biblical narrative regarding her as 'opaque'. Maddox (1987: 17) clearly sees Tamar as the story's hero, defined as 'one who represents God's concern for justice and shalom'.

25. Alter 1981: 7.

26. Maddox (1987: 15) calls Tamar a 'feminist foremother' who overcame and subverted compounded oppression. Not only was she, as all women, 'dependent upon a required relationship to a male', but also a childless widow oppressed by the levirate law and Judah's failure to keep it, with no legal protection or recourse.

27. Gunn and Fewell (1993: 38) keenly note: 'To get out of her widow's clothes permanently [Tamar] must put them aside temporarily. Thus her changing of clothes, which neatly frames her dangerous deception, is symbolic of her larger goal.'

28. Van Wolde 1997: 9; Gunn and Fewell 1993: 45.

hard labor (pun intended) of birthing, and the honor of naming my babies.[29] (Do men comfort themselves with the notion that giving birth, because it is 'natural', is by any means passive? I invite you men into the delivery room for a bit of an eye-opening!) But here at least I am in good company with no less than the mother of Moses,[30] a nameless woman whose narrative is overshadowed by the active midwives of her day.

I had such a fleeting moment of glory! Even when I was publicly vindicated, Judah's confession was ambiguous and didn't completely satisfy me. He didn't even speak it directly to me! If he had, I might have been able to forgive everything right then and there. But I suspect that even in his apparent humility he was still keeping up appearances. He is always the 'smooth-talker' in public, but you should have heard his coarseness in the privacy of our exchange! I should like to know what he really meant by saying, 'She is more righteous than I'.[31] If he meant (and he has given various statements to the interviewers who have quoted him recently)[32] that I was more 'in the right' or 'had more right' to do what I did than he had to do what he did, I think he is right (that is, correct!). Everyone generally agrees on this point, and it does mean something to me, because at least it justifies the means I used to achieve my end, which was good.[33] It also acknowledges that he was indebted to me,[34] so that by giving me sons he did not do me any 'favor' but only fulfilled through his own person that which he was obligated to fulfill through his son Shelah anyway (but had been avoiding; yea, even intentionally deceiving me—

29. Menn 1997: 33-34.

30. See also Pseudo-Philo's implicit comparison in his reference to Tamar in the Exodus context in Van der Horst 1993.

31. The root of the word righteous (*ṣdq*) appears in a form here (38.26) that is unique in the Torah (Hayes 1995: 65).

32. See Hayes 1995. He discusses interpretations and variations of Judah's confession in nine different sources, including ancient and non-canonical. Different implications of the confession range from a simple admission of fatherhood to the relative righteousness of him and Tamar to the whole incident being God's responsibility. Apparently some patriarchal exegetes were uncomfortable with the idea of a Canaanite prostitute surpassing their forefather in righteousness (which reminds me of some New Testament texts regarding the Pharisees' estimation of 'unclean' women!).

33. Mathewson (1989: 380 n. 38) states that the basic meaning of 'righteous' is conformity to a standard—'in this case the social custom and duty of levirate marriage'.

34. Judah didn't realize the extent of his indebtedness to Tamar: 'the privilege of founding the Davidic line and giving his name to an entire people' (Frankel 1996: 79).

though he didn't 'see' me, I saw right through his scheme thinly veiled by an implied promise).

But I wish he had been brave and humble enough to mean more than just this narrow, legal sense of the word 'righteous'.[35] I longed to hear him truly confess that I am more morally 'upright' than he is, that I did 'righter' in the eyes of Yhwh. That's how it clearly appears to me, anyway. He was the one blocking not only the fulfillment of the levirate law which he owed to me, but also the continuation of the line of his tribe, which he owed to the Israelite people.[36] He was the stalemate, the impasse.[37] Funny, he must have thought of me as the 'stale mate', the one with whom life cannot go on. He feared I killed his sons! He was totally unaware or in denial of his sons' wickedness and God's hand in their deaths.[38] He was not only 'less righteous' than I but he was actually in a state of sin or rebellion to God and God's people. When he said I am more righteous than he, he made it sound like he is righteous too. He made it sound like we were playing the same game on the same board, only this time I happened to beat him. Furthermore, he only gave the partial truth for his 'less righteousness': that he withheld his son from me. What about a more gritty accounting of what he actually did? 'His' son was supposed to be my husband and the father of my children. Was he merely hanging on to his beloved possession or was he coveting and stealing what was rightfully mine and yours, fellow Jews? Was he a bereaved and protective father, or a self-centered lawbreaker? Not to mention the sexual immorality that *no one* seems to care about![39]

35. *Ṣdq* is a legal term: it means she has presented the convincing evidence (Alter 1996: 223).

36. Brueggemann's main contribution to the discussion of Gen. 38 lies in his insight here: the moral critique of this chapter is not sexual sin but damage to the community (esp. of the people of faith). He compares Judah to Achan—a descendant of Judah—who is punished for serving his self-interest at the expense of the community by stealing what is God's (Josh. 7). He sees Judah's son as something Judah must give not solely for Tamar but for the future and solidarity of the community (Brueggemann 1982: 310-11).

37. Menn 1997: 21, 35.

38. That Judah was unaware—or chose to ignore—his sons' evil is widely accepted (Frankel 1996: 75; Van Wolde 1997: 13). Stigers calls him 'spiritually unperceptive' (Mathewson 1989: 378-79). Gunn and Fewell (1993: 36) astutely observe that 'after all, he and his brothers suffered no consequences for their dealings with Joseph'.

39. Lev. 18.15 and 20.12 prohibit father-in-law–daughter-in-law sexual relations, which are punishable by death for both parties. However, Judah's sexual escapade is

Though the Torah doesn't outlaw prostitution, Yhwh forbade his children to have sexual relations with or to become 'sacred' prostitutes of the Canaanite cult variety[40] which Judah decorously made me out to be in his public search.[41] I risked everything to obtain an identity and future security for myself, not to mention fulfill social custom and God's laws, and he gave away everything—his identity and credit cards—for nothing more than a frisk![42] Of course he wouldn't have allowed anyone to discover this embarrassing fact unless I had forced the confession. He was always concerned about his appearances. People are telling me I should be exulting in the triumph of my plan, and the public vindication of Judah's confession (not to mention the avoidance of impending death!). But I must admit I am left unsatisfied at the deeper level; a confession forced doesn't have the same sense of sincerity as one borne out of conviction and remorse.[43] 'The Lord has had mercy on me, a sinner!' would have been more to my liking, and more realistic to his position, I think. However, as Judah proved not to be the judge of me in the end, so I shall prove not to be the judge of him. It seems that the Lord has indeed had mercy on him, and who knows the state of one's heart but the Lord? Let me find my fulfillment not in Judah's humiliation but through my sons, my community, and my God.

That reminds me of another point. Some people have been speculating about my heritage. Am I Canaanite or am I a daughter of Abraham?[44]

---

told without censure with regard to these laws. Is it because this incest law assumes that the daughter-in-law's husband is still alive (in other words, Judah ceased to be Tamar's father-in-law after Er's death)? The text reads otherwise, making the in-law relationship explicit even after Er's death, which is evidenced by the titles used for both Judah and Tamar.

40. Frankel 1996: 77.

41. In Judah's third-party public search for Tamar, he inquires after a $q^e d\bar{e}\check{s}\hat{a}$ (a cult prostitute) rather than a $z\bar{o}n\hat{a}$ (a garden-variety whore) which had been his private estimation of Tamar upon seeing her by the gate of Enaim (Bird 1997: 206-207; Alter 1981: 7; Gunn and Fewell 1993: 41).

42. Frankel 1996: 77; Alter 1996: 221.

43. Gunn and Fewell (1993: 43) call Judah's statement a 'concession' rather than a confession: he speaks indirectly, doesn't apologize or ask forgiveness, is concerned only to impress the public and diverts attention from the issue of his promiscuity to the legalities of levirate marriage ['for I did not give her my son Shelah'] in order to offer a lame self-justification to which men of his day would have been sympathetic.

44. See Johnson 1969: 270-72, 'Appendix 4: The Ancestry of Tamar in Later Jewish Tradition'.

Inquiring minds want to know! Yes, I know Israelites are very concerned about the purity of their genes and culture, for good reasons (obedience and avoiding 'pagan temptations') and for bad (ethnocentrism). Have you heard the rumors that I seduced Yhwh himself into 'entering me'? Now that's a thought! As if Yhwh were Judah…

Well, let's let that issue come to a rest. I am a granddaughter of Noah, a daughter of Shem, from whom our father of faith himself was descended.[45] Why else, unless I were the daughter of a priest, would I be liable to death by burning for harlotry (Lev. 21.9)? Even if I were a Canaanite, then I would be the prototype for Raḥab and Ruth after me, foreigners who sided with the promises and the people of Yhwh at their own risk—and for their faith, Yhwh made them his own. But lest there be any remaining doubt, Yhwh has indisputably settled the matter. He has made me his daughter by making me the mother of a son who will beget his own son in due time. I am one of only four women—a number symbolizing completion, totality, solidarity[46]—mentioned in the genealogy of the Messiah according to Matthew.[47] By my actions I am 100 per cent Jew[48]… O heck, I'm a more faithful Jew than the eponymous Jew himself! Whereas he seemed cavalier about the promises and commands of God, I hung onto them as if my life depended upon them.[49] And that leads me back to my original beef: why am I such a subverted character in this story?[50] Is this another one of those incidents of 'patriarchal bias' that so many women have been writing in to complain about lately? If things don't change in your literary

45. Ulanov 1993: 98 n. 2; Johnson 1969: 154, 271-72.

46. Ulanov 1993: 10-11.

47. 'Looked at causally, the four female ancestors of Jesus show the long-omitted female elements that insist on being included in our lives and that in their acceptance secure the line of David. This shows that Christ as the new Messiah will bring with him not merely acceptance but willing inclusion of the female elements of being' (Ulanov 1993: 6).

48. Whether or not commentators stake their claim on Tamar's heritage as Canaanite or Jewish (they fall equally strongly on both sides; the text itself is silent), there is widespread agreement that her actions align her with God's chosen people. According to Frankel (1996: 75), Tamar 'submits her deeds as pledge of her citizenship'.

49. Gunn and Fewell 1993: 38.

50. Menn (1997: 15) proposes that the 'central issue driving the narrative consists of the transition from one generation to the next'. Tamar is hence relegated to a reproductive usefulness, serving male interests narratively.

world, you might be facing a class-action discrimination suit here fairly soon!

Letter 4: From Ruth

I was thrilled to read the story of Tamar and Judah published last week. How often have I been told that I remind someone of her![51] I finally see why. We were both widows, we were both sent back to our parents' home by our parent-in-law, our stories constitute the only narrative examples of levirate law in context and enactment,[52] we are both foreigners who bound ourselves through persistence, sexuality and ingenuity to the Jewish people, and we are both ancestors of King David, though we disappear as mothers after our sons' births.[53] We are kindred spirits, I think! I have just now finished up drafting some notes for my own biography, which I hope will be published soon (high aspirations, I know), and I have decided to make a special point of connecting myself to this amazing woman by locating my husband, Boaz, in the lineage of Perez. Like Tamar and Rahab and Uriah's wife, I am so grateful to have been 'grafted in' to the tree of life and the family of God as an 'honorary daughter'.[54] Undoubtedly you are aware of the Israelite enmity with the Moabites and the prohibition of this people to enter the temple of Yhwh. And yet I am a Moabite, which makes David and Jesus, perhaps the two greatest worshippers of all time, partly Moabite! As women used so graciously by God in the fulfillment of His promises, we serve as a hope and a symbol for the nations outside the covenant who will be brought into it through our own flesh and blood in the form of the Messiah.[55] Our Messiah will rule, redeem and reconcile

---

51. 'Ruth is a second Tamar' (Lacocque 1990: 105).

52. Lacocque 1990: 93-94.

53. For a full discussion of the intertextuality between the Tamar and Ruth narratives, see Van Wolde 1997: 8-28.

54. Cf. Ulanov 1993: 1-19, especially the introduction. Also Johnson 1969: 152-55 on the four women [Tamar, Rahab, Ruth and Bathsheba] in Jesus' genealogy. Why these four non-Jewish women, which include two harlots and one adulteress, as opposed to the traditional 'four ancestral mothers' [Sarah, Rebekah, Rachel and Leah], who are more 'innocuous'? Two hypotheses are that their inclusion symbolizes the inclusion in general of sinners and Gentiles into Israel/the Church, or polemically to introduce blots on David's genealogy (154-55).

55. Lacocque (1990: 84-116) draws parallels between Ruth and Gen. 38. The word *hesed* (steadfast love) in Ruth describes intimacy between God and his people, rather than being universalistic; it is scandalous that an outsider (a Moabitess) is a model of this.

Jews, Moabites, Canaanites and all people. Could this be what it means that we shall be 'saved through childbearing'? In other words, that childbearing is the means through which salvation has entered the world? We women and we 'outsiders' have been pressed into the center of God's own history.[56] Hallelujah!

Letter 5: From Lot's daughters

We thank our dear friend and daughter Ruth for her most encouraging letter. And as her ancestors, we feel we too must make a plea to the people of Israel for understanding and acceptance. How long has our story been obscured and ignored[57] or, even worse, used judgmentally as an example of immorality and the 'breakdown of the family'.[58] From the caves above Zoar, where 'the door is dust that kept us in' and where 'frost that hardens flesh has made us old',[59] we have called out: is anybody there? ('is anybody there?' echoes hollow over the plains stretching to the sea). If we told you who we were, you would not recognize us by our names, as they have been completely ignored. Like the women before us, you know us only in relation to the males in our life, our father and our sons. In these three ways—through geography, anonymity, and patriarchy—and in many more, we have been pushed to the very edges of human existence. First of all, as descendants of Lot, we were split off from the central people of God (that is to say, Abraham's line) and the blessings thereof because of a separation over a land dispute. Were it not for Abraham's intercession, might we too be ashes right now? Then, as the daughters of the consummate host, Lot, we were pushed to bottom-most rung of the social ladder when he offered us up (like a plate of appetizers!) to the violent men of Sodom. Some try to defend his honor by claiming hospitality is the

---

56. Van Wolde (1997: 27) proposes that not only are the Tamar and Ruth narratives to be read along gender lines, but also in terms of 'insideness' and 'outsideness'.

57. I found a remarkable scarcity of commentary on this passage regarding Lot's daughters in Gen. 19.30-38, especially compared to the abundance of discussion on the previous 29 verses leading up to the destruction of Sodom. Brueggemann (1982: 176-77) offers one paragraph in his commentary, minimizing it as 'a saga not related to our main consideration' (similar to his comments on Gen. 38). Surprisingly he concludes that Lot and his daughters, while designated as 'other peoples' (i.e. non-Abrahamic), are at the same time 'clearly treated as members of the family of promise'.

58. Hewett 1989: 241. He describes the daughters' behavior as 'choosing perversity out of moral ignorance'.

59. Barfoot 1988: 23 (phrases from a poem about Lot's daughters).

utmost value and virtue.[60] We certainly did not perceive him as 'hospitable' to us! At first we ran and hid, but when he found us, we beat his chest, crying and yelling, 'Why, daddy, why? How could you do this to us?' He pleaded with us and lamely insisted that he didn't think the monstrous crowd would accept his offer anyway, which is why he felt 'free' to do it. But what if they had? Could he even conceive of the terror of the possibilities of rape, torture and even death legitimated by his words, 'do to them as you please'? We understand first-hand how our poor cousin felt not much later, awaiting seemingly certain death atop that cold stone slab, terrified and powerless at his father's bidding.[61] (At least he had the consolation of his father's faithfulness to Elohim, which we did not.) Like Isaac, our lives were spared. Unlike him, our dignity was not. And though our bodies were spared from destruction—twice!—it was so hard to recall the relief and gratitude for life amidst the fiery pain that ensued. We lost so much, tragically and terribly, in one panicked swoop: our older sisters and brothers-in-law,[62] our home and town, our friends, comfort, safety and laughter, our own dear mother. In our isolation, like Noah's family after the great flood, we felt utterly alone, as if the continuation of life on earth were up to us.[63] Could we let our family die, one by one, until the three of us lay rotting in a cave, waiting to be devoured by wild animals? With this hopelessness and desperation, we did a desperate thing. Some accuse us of dishonoring our father by intoxicating him and, for all practical purposes, raping him[64] (yes, woman as sexual aggressor is not a popular thought). But hadn't he already made it clear to us that our sexuality was meant to suit his purposes and to preserve himself?[65] We did

60. Elliott 1961: 134. He goes on to say that Lot 'cannot be blamed too much for his willingness to sacrifice his daughters', giving the rationale that it was the lesser of two evils, since women were merely regarded as property ('chattel'). Alter (1996: 85 n. 8) disagrees, viewing Lot's offer as 'shocking', and 'too patly explained as the reflex of an Ancient Near East code in which the sacredness of the host–guest bond took precedence over all other obligations'.

61. Maddox (1987: 16) emphasizes the 'decision of the male family head is taken without question'.

62. Alter 1996: 87 n. 14.

63. Frankel (1996: 88) mentions Noah–Lot parallels. Also Elliott 1961: 137.

64. The Hebrew verb 'to lie with' (*škb*) is coarse (not euphemistic, as it seems to modern-day readers) and is used here in such a way as to construe forcefulness. The same also applies to Potiphar's wife's urgings toward Joseph in Gen. 39, and Amnon's urgings toward his sister Tamar in 2 Sam. 13. See Alter 1996: 90.

65. Frankel 1996: 25.

not lie with our father in a vindictive spirit. We used the one thing we had left, our bodies, to grow within us a hope for our future and to redeem our father's lost honor.[66] Can we be blamed (and are we blamed) for taking our destinies into our control and using the remnant of power we had?

People say we are condemned for incest,[67] but isn't it at least interesting that the law never mentions the specific prohibition of a father lying with a daughter?[68] Oh the whole sexual ethics thing is so complicated by the compromise of God to our sinfulness in the first place.[69] Let's not even get into the whole discussion of the 'double standard' for men and women which Tamar's story so perfectly exemplifies.[70] No, we do not want to be angry victims nor do we want pity. We are not trying to defend ourselves. Neither do we ask for popular opinion either to justify or judge us. Because we mothered the Moabite and Ammonite nations, long-standing enemies of Israel, this is taken as a 'sign' of God's disapproval of our actions.[71] Our offspring are cast out of the temple and out of the Israelite chosen. But then again, Ruth was a Moabite and a progenitor of Jesus. The Chosen One of Israel has finally healed that original split between our

66. Alter (1996: 85 n. 8) sees Lot's unwitting participation in his daughters' loss of virginity as 'measure for measure justice meted out for his rash offer' of them to the Sodomites earlier in the chapter. I can only guess that this is because a daughter's honor (her virginity and marriageability) directly corresponds to her father's honor. Both honors are lost twice in Gen. 19, first by verbal offering-up and secondly by the incestuous act.

67. Both sons' names are etymologized to refer to incest: Moab is construed as 'from the father' and Ammon is construed as 'my own kinsman's son' (Alter 1996: 90). He notes, however, that the narrator of this chapter withholds evaluation of the 'incestuous enterprise', and that the story could either be used to prove the purity of these two peoples, or to cast a shadow over two of Israel's enemies.

68. Hewett 1989: 241.

69. For example, polygamy, divorce, concubines and prostitution were all cultural givens and not outlawed by the Torah, though none of those fit into God's ideal intention for man, woman and marriage in Gen. 1 and 2.

70. Day (1989: 79) charges that prostitution and fornication share a 'fundamentally female profile' despite necessary male participation. Recall Judah's hasty condemnation of Tamar for something in which he too had partaken; culturally his condemnation of her actions was just or appropriate, whereas she did not have the same power of proclamation over him. Day notes that the book of Hosea turns men's accusations of 'fallen women' against themselves: 'You [male Israel] are that woman!' (1989: 89). See also Gunn and Fewell 1993: 42. For a fuller discussion of sexual ethics in ancient Israel (especially relating to the Tamar story), see Bird 1997: 197-236.

71. Elliott 1961: 136.

father and the father of faith.[72] So, if we can be condemned by our off-spring, can we then be redeemed by our offspring?

Letter 6: From Israelite Women
We, Society of Israelite Ladies for Equality in Narrative, Culture, Education and Dignity (S.I.L.E.N.C.E.D.), read the letter from Tamar the other day and we felt compelled to respond. We needed to make public our statement of agreement with her and support of her.

We all have a lot in common with her, probably more than she knows...

Each in our own way, and yet in strikingly similar ways, have all been silenced and minimized, forced to repeat those mythic 'disappearing acts'. Here is some of what our members have to say regarding the topic at hand:

I am Sarah, one of the oldest members of this society. I really know the suffering and dehumanization Tamar has gone through regarding this whole identity deception thing. I was not once but twice pawned off to some king or ruler as my husband's sister (and I regretfully admit to having supported this plan) instead of insisting upon my rightful and honorable place as his wife. We are the 'mother and father of faith', mind you, though not much was evidenced in this trickery! In being turned over freely and deceitfully to Pharaoh (ch. 12) and Abimelech (ch. 20), I lost not only my dignity and integrity but my identity. And why? Because my husband Abraham was afraid of harm coming to himself on account of my surpassing beauty. So a woman's beauty gives a man the right to take her from another man without regard to her desires and to her relationship with these men? (I find it interesting that we have never yet read of a case in which a woman 'took' a man from another woman on account of his surpassing handsomeness! It seems men move more freely between and across social and relational boundaries regarding gender and act as 'female-brokers'; women are more constrained by these prescribed boundaries and are acted upon and broken.) Is beauty, then, a form of power—one which must be managed lest it get out of control? Having my real identity thrust back upon me (the poor deceived ones didn't ask for their affliction), twice I emerged as myself, but not unscathed in my own self-esteem and not unscathed in my marital happiness, either.[73] Abe and I really had some rough times working that one out! Eventually, we were

---

72. Frankel 1996: 79.

73. Frankel (1996: 27) says of Sarah and Abraham: 'Even a mock adultery can permanently scar its victims'.

both able to forgive each other when we realized and confessed that our fear had overtaken our trust of each other and of Yhwh, and that I had been the scapegoat who paid the price.

I am Rebekah. I too was passed off by my husband as his sister to Abimelech (ch. 26) for the same reasons: my beauty, his fear of death. (Like father, like son!) But I can relate to Tamar on a couple of other counts: I am also the mother of twins, of which the younger usurped the older, and I am also an author of deception devised to work out God's plans and promises. I worked out my plans after the birth of my sons, not before. Sometimes our men get in the way a bit, don't they? I mean, the father–son bond (between Isaac and Esau in my case, and between Judah and Shelah in yours) was really a deterrent to the working out of God's plan. Personally, I think this whole emphasis our culture places on sons, and on first-borns in particular, is overblown and not really godly. I think He shows this time and again with the blessing and choosing of the younger brothers.[74] At any rate, I thank God that His promises have not only to do with land, which our men could try—and they so desperately do—to possess by force and physical might, but also with descendants. In this gracious way, God has inextricably and irreplaceably involved us women of Israel in the destiny of Israel and the destiny of God on earth. We need not just sons of promise but daughters to be the next generation of mothers. Aren't the men of the lineage of the promise also the precious little babes we birthed and nursed and the strapping young lads we married and loved and influenced with our love? It is our place, then, in marriage and in the family, to exercise our part in our people's history. It is our every right and even our mandate to use the position and power we have in Israel's history to make what needs to happen, happen. If we must channel our influence through our children or through our 'deceit' (I prefer to call it 'imagination') or through our sexuality, because we do not have a public forum to speak out for ourselves straightforwardly, then let it be so. We will not stand by passively and watch God's word go unfulfilled when we could have done something about it any way we can. Where men can afford the luxury of being unoriginal and traditional sometimes, we women cannot. We refuse to be labeled 'crafty'—when what we are forced to do is be incredibly creative and resourceful thinkers and problem-solvers!

74. Goldin (1977: 28). See n. 13 for further discussion.

I, Rachel, stand with Tamar in her experience of powerlessness and betrayal. Like her, I was deprived by my father of the man who was supposed to be my husband. No matter how I pleaded and cried on my knees with sobs too deep for words, my older sister was given over to my true love in a calculating, manipulative move. Yes, unlike Tamar, I did eventually get my husband, but not without having to endure the jealous rivalry of my sister for the rest of my life. But like her, I was an outsider, spurned for my childlessness. Oh, what a double pain, for me not to have children while my sister and my husband were popping them out like flatcakes! The shame I endured, I feel it must have been greater than the stigma of being a widow. Like Tamar, I understand the hopelessness and desperation that precipitates the demand for children, whether that demand be verbal (as it was in my case) or behavioral (as it was in hers). For we feel so acutely what it is to be women without children. It's like being without an identity ('I'm so-and-so's mom'), without hope for future security (who will provide for us in our old age?), without status or position. We feel we have nothing to offer the community, and no part in history. Without children, we make a name neither for ourselves nor for another. They are a life-and-death matter for us! We spend our lives for them, and we die for them too, in ways both literary and literal: Tamar ceased to exist in the narrative after the birth of her sons, and I passed away giving birth to my youngest son, Benjamin.

Leah here. You know, I was reflecting how much Tamar and I have in common, not the least of which is Judah. The son who came out of me went into her so that sons may come out of her. And, like her, I too tricked the father of my children into lying with me by the use of a veil disguising my true identity. I know the pain of rejection, of being put 'on hold', as if something is distasteful or repulsive about us. We were not wanted for who we were, and so we got what we wanted by pretending to be someone else. Jacob and Judah were so surprised to find out our true identities (I wish I had had my camera with me to capture the expression on his face 'the morning after'!), and boy, were they ever angry and disappointed and ashamed when they found out. At least Jacob had the decency to commit to me and take me as a real wife, whereas Judah 'never knew [Tamar] again'. (Just between you and me, honey, I don't think he ever really knew her *at all*,[75] except in the narrowest euphemistic use of the word! It was his

75. A recurring characteristic of Judah is seeing without knowing: his sons, his daughter-in-law, himself (Gunn and Fewell 1993: 44; Van Wolde 1997: 15). Ironic

loss.) I know what it's like to feel the 'second-rate' citizen. I so longed for a husband who reciprocated my love; I died a thousand deaths of jealousy every time I saw the twinkle in Jacob's eye when he talked to Rachel or smiled at her in a way that he never did with me. I know Rachel was sickly jealous of my children, but I don't think she realized what she did have that was more precious than gold: the heart of her husband! Sure, I had so many children by Jacob, including the first-born son, I should have had mountains of honor and favor. But you know, ladies, I don't really believe our children buy us status and privilege in the way our hearts most long for it. Children mean a lot but they never really replace our own selves. At least, speaking from my own experience, I wanted to be loved for me, for who I am as a woman. I'm sure Tamar must have felt this way in the wicked embrace of Onan, the one who had sex with her but never made love to her.[76] I know what it feels like to be the object by which a man merely fulfills a familial obligation—and it hurts. I would cry myself to sleep so many nights. How long will we have to wait for mutual, loving relationships, the abolition of polygamy and utilitarian marriage? Which is better, to be married but the less-favored wife, or to be scandalously twice-widowed with no forthcoming prospects? Ladies, there must be another choice!

Gentlewomen, it's clear that we've all been victims of this editorial process called life. We've been left out and written out, disappeared, died, and been overshadowed (and not by the Holy Spirit!). Only a few of our stories have been told, and even then only in part, and only from the point of view of the men to whom we related or the men to whom the story was relayed. The whole of the people of Israel, and I dare say the whole world, has suffered and suffers still from the permanent lack and loss of our distinctive voices. Something essential about the character of God and the image of God has been tragically lost. For our own sake and for the sake of humanity, no longer should we allow what men say about us to be the final word!

wordplay may be at work in 'the entrance to Enaim' (the gate where he sees a prostitute), which means 'opening of the eyes' (Gunn and Fewell 1993: 39). Tamar will eventually open his eyes! Of additional interest is the play on the name 'Timnah', the place of the sheep-shearing, which comes from 'reckoning'—so was Judah on the way to a reckoning?

76. Ironically the meaning of the Onan's name, the one who refused to impregnate Tamar, is 'virility' (Lacocque 1990: 104).

Letter 7: From Eve

I agreed with much that my fellow colleagues of the Society put forth, and deeply sympathized with their pain. Still, I felt compelled to respond because I felt I must not let us women get away with something that has no constructive value and devastating effects. I have suffered from it personally, as its first victim and its second perpetrator, and that thing is blame. We're going all the way back to the garden here, beloved *'iššâ*, if we let the last word be not of man but of woman's pointing the finger and passing the buck! My exhortation is that we all have to take responsibility for ourselves! It is true that men have kept women under their collective thumb in almost every way (that dreaded 'P' word). They are responsible for their repentance and subsequent restitution-making efforts to woman. On the other hand, some women have managed to squirm out from under that thumb (though we have to endure that disagreeable label, 'subversive'). These are the women who change things for all of us, including the men. They are the brave, the risk-takers, the vocal or active ones who resist suppression. Tamar is one of these, and is in some ways a model for faithfulness. No doubt you are all aware of Pseudo-Philo's unprecedented and unsurpassed praise of her alone as 'our mother', a title of honor rivaling 'our father' Abraham's.[77] What can we learn from her? The world may be a certain way, but it doesn't have to be! We have power, and not just in our beauty, sexuality and children, either! In our ideas, our audacity, our boldness and strategizing, our courage and convictions.

We all know that Gen. 3.16 is not indeed a 'curse' by which we must suffer under male domination[78] (no, Yhwh, Blessed be 'He', is not an oppressive male, contrary to popular belief![79]). Rather, it is a prophetic description of how we as women abdicate our God-given right, even mandate, to exercise dominion in and over the earth. I am the first to confess, for I am the first to sin. I trespassed God's dominion by disobeying his command. I passed on to you, my dear daughters, the unfortunate legacy

---

77. There is no parallel to this appellation in biblical or early Jewish literature for any woman from the Bible; it elevates Tamar to matriarchal (or patriarchal?) status (van der Horst 1993: 301).

78. In Gen. 3, Trible 1978: 126-28 notes that God cursed the serpent directly, the man indirectly, and the woman not at all. Feminist commentators (e.g. Maddox 1987: 17) generally agree that 3.16 is descriptive, not prescriptive.

79. Ulanov 1993: 23-24 discusses the image of 'father' God as metaphorical; God is not sexual.

of the loss of personal dominion as my just consequence.[80] I cannot possibly express the depths of my regret and pain for the situation I have put you all in. I can only try to do now what I have learned the hard way, and that is, to take responsibility for my own actions. We compensate for our loss of power with excessive sociability (and don't we all know how we are prone to gossip!), a desire to be in and maintain harmonious relationships at any cost.[81] We have been intimidated and afraid to speak out or take our place of authority for fear of 'hurting someone's feelings'. Well, harmony, schmarmony! It's not that we want to buy into the vicious, depersonalizing competition of a power struggle at the expense of intimacy and friendship (that's Adam's legacy to you men: increased dominance but decreased sociability—a different but not a better picture overall, if you ask me). However, it is time we exercised a little more of our natural dominion and a little less of our natural sociability. Men have wronged us and we are victims personally and corporately of abuses of power. But we have been passive accomplices of our own silence. It's time to speak out, and I thank the editor for doing his part in allowing our voices to be heard now.

Conclusion: From the Editor

I appreciate all of the discussion and various points of view expressed in this section over the last several issues. I will try as much as possible to take them into account when compiling the stories for The Book. It is clear that everyone has strong opinions, and insights and perspective that come from their own life. Let me be the first to admit that I, too, have my own lens through which I see things.[82] I cannot possibly be true to everyone at once. And so I will disappoint many or all of you at some time or another. And yet, that is the risk that Yhwh took when he entrusted me with the job

---

80. Trible 1978: 128.

81. Van Leeuwen (1990: 44-47) presents the concepts of 'accountable dominion' and 'sociability' as being natural, God-given gifts to both women and men which have been distorted in specific ways because of the nature of Adam and Eve's sins. Eve violated dominion (God's command) and therefore will be dominated; Adam violated sociability (listening to his wife about eating the fruit) and therefore will suffer diminished social capacity. Enmeshment and domination are the resultant sinful tendencies, respectfully. The tricky part, warns Van Leeuwen, is that women's sin more often 'masquerades as virtue'. Shalom includes men and women in right relationship, exercising both aspects of power in proportion.

82. For example, Menn (1997: 2) points out that different interpretations of Gen. 38 lead to different foci.

and the calling to write all these things down for the people of Israel and for the generations to come. I suppose he could have recorded our collective history directly onto a stone tablet or some such thing (just a crazy thought). But in entrusting me and all of us to the process, he allowed room for discrepancy at best, and error and selfish propaganda at worst. I shall have to account for the writing and editing job I do; I pray His mercy upon me, that He should use to His good purposes whatever I produce with my best effort and His divine inspiration.

My exhortation to all of you is to let the stories provoke us to thought, to challenge ourselves and to reflect, and most of all to relate with resonance. Instead of scrambling to categorize, systematize, 'figure out' and evaluate others' lives (especially as compared to ourselves and our moral standards),[83] I wish we could just sit with the ambiguity and rich-ness and complexity of the stories. Just as no two people are identical, so Yhwh never seems to do anything exactly the same twice. We can never, and we must never, reduce the Unknowable into a formula or a status quo. We don't know the answers to life (especially another's life), and most often we don't even know the questions! Why do we so desperately want to have the final word on what someone else's life has meant, whether they did 'right or wrong', 'good or bad'? We shall not be the knower or the judge of this—remember that tree that the first of us were forbidden to eat? Let's let His work in us, through us, with us and despite us continue to lead us ever on to increasing intimacy and boldness with the One who made us, in gratitude, obedience, humility and faith.

83. 'While reading Genesis 38 through a lens of morality raises serious questions about the appropriateness of Judah and Tamar's actions, the biblical narrative itself does little to resolve these questions' (Menn 1997: 42). Brueggemann (1982: 309) warns that our interpretation 'must not introduce moral dimensions alien to the text itself'.

WIDE GAPS, NARROW ESCAPES:
I AM KNOWN AS RAHAB, THE BROAD

Athalya Brenner

Many critics, and readers are devoted to understanding the Bible 'as it was', that is, they reconstruct an implied audience, an implied milieu, an implied culture, an implied religion, an implied theology, an implied author with which to understand biblical texts. *Au contraire,* I often think. What would biblical narratives look like if rewritten with modern and postmodern concerns in mind, in addition to concerns voiced by contemporary Bible and literature scholars? Such concerns might include issues of authorship and readership, for instance. Or of literary theory, such as narratology (Bal 1985) or gap-filling (Sternberg 1985). Or the links between nationalism and group and individual identity, or religion and war. Or ethnicity. Or history and historiography. And, ultimately, feminism and liberation from oppression. What would happen, in short, if we turn the tables and retell a biblical story, using our own intellectual and scholarly tools and voicing our own concerns rather than those of the implied biblical author? The following narrative is an attempt at a rewrite of a biblical narrative, focused on the narratologically prominent figure in this story, from her viewpoint, by way of redressing the balance, narrated in the first-person mode. A fictitious biography, the revis[it]ed story of Joshua 2 and 6, the story of Rahab and the Israelite spies.

My real name is… It doesn't matter what it is. I *do* have a proper name. But it's been forgotten, or suppressed. My nickname, the one that supplanted my real name until the real name has been deleted from all the official documentation is 'Rahab'. Now this, in Hebrew, means the 'wide' or 'broad' [one]. Please do not think for a moment that this 'wideness' refers to my being far from slim. No, although that might be true as well: even in those far-off days I never lacked for food in my childhood, being a member of the upper mercantile, landholding class and later an enterprising professional woman. There is a sexual pun here: those of you with a little bit of Hebrew and imagination are right. From antiquity on, this is how I was known.[1] The Hebrew scribes who wrote down what they imagined as 'my' story preferred to introduce me by that nickname. They often suppressed women's names in their stories: this praxis made the woman figures seem less real, less important.[2] A basic literary technique that suited the writers' and scribes' purposes.[3] The sages of that motley group, members of which wrote stories later incorporated into their sacred writings, enjoyed the vulgar connotations. This is how I am known, although later generations elevated me to the status of matriarch. And I, from where I am, from where I've been all this time (I refuse to divulge my exact age; female wiles, so what? Stereotypic, so what?), I can laugh and cry in equal measures. But let me tell my story from my own perspective, even some of the suppressed parts, in the order of events I remember well. As they happened. From *my* viewpoint, rather than from theirs. And if I rewrite history here—who am I to deny that a little bit of that will occur, it always does—so be it.

I was, am (my *Nachleben* in the canonized literatures of the belief systems that later came to be known as Judaism and Christianity allows me the present tense) an ordinary upper middle-class girl. My mother was a housewife and mother, my father was in the textile business.[4] I grew up with the smell of flax and expensive cloth, international trade, political

1.   *Sif. Zut.* 10: 'Rabbi Yehudah says, she had four names of disrepute. Her name, Raḥab the whore, says it all. Another thing, Raḥab the whore because she fornicated with the city people from within, and with the bandits from without, since it is said that "her house was in the wall" and "she sits in the wall" (Josh. 2.15). Another thing, Raḥab the whore since she was a Canaanite, and there were no more evil and wicked people than the Canaanites. Another thing, Raḥab the whore since she was from the people of Jericho, those about whom it is written that they should be demolished and banned (Deut. 20.17)' (my translation AB).

2.   See Meyers 1994, esp. 96-99.

3.   See Reinhartz 1994.

4.   While it is certainly true that processing flax may have been a woman's job, it is perhaps surprising to find raw flax on a bordello's roof in quantities sufficient for hiding one or two persons (Josh. 2.6)—even when the flax is needed for the plot, even when a realistic picture should not be expected. We may therefore assume, by way of filling a gap, that Raḥab was somehow familiar with flax processing as a profession or trade. A similar echo underlies, perhaps, the insistence of some Jewish midrashic sources that a guild of white linen workers, mentioned in 1 Chron. 4.21 as a family ('house of byssus work'), was descended from Raḥab (*Sif. Zut.* 10; *Ruth R.* 2; and more). And see below.

gossip. We had lands and a town house inside the walled city. I had brothers and sisters; I was the eldest. I was born and raised in Jericho, an oasis, a very ancient city near the Dead Sea not far from Jerusalem.[5] This town is nowadays Palestinian; it used to be Israeli; before that it was Arab; in my time it was labelled Canaanite. My childhood was uneventful. I was an obedient child, good-looking, pleasant. Loved my siblings and honoured my parents, as prescribed in our law tablets (and theirs). Looked forward to a stable life like my mother's, with a husband and children, eventually grandchildren, under my own palm trees (neither the proverbial vine not the fig trees grow well in our immediate geotopographic neighbourhood). When was that? Ah, about thirteen to twelve hundred years before the man Jesus, described as a descendant of mine, was born.[6] Or something like this.

But history intervened. There were waves of invaders from the northeast and the east, from the so-called Fertile Crescent and the Asian steppes. Hungry, unruly mobs of desert and margin shepherd-warriors would descend on our arable lands and unwalled towns, the desert-encircled agricultural hinterland of our marvellously cultured, ancient, walled city. They would demolish or capture everything in sight. They also, sometimes, had the nasty habit of killing all males, sparing women and children only; or killing all human beings in the name of their religion: on such occasions, taking captives and keeping them alive was not for them.[7] They did make an exception in the case of female virgins, though, especially the young and beautiful ones.[8] But let's not dwell on the fate of those: too unpleasant to recall, although these virgins' lives were spared.

This process of slow infiltration, in waves, from the east happened over a few decades,[9] with monotonous regularity, usually in the spring and summer and harvest time. Inflation and scarcity of food became commonplace. Gradually, my father lost most of his merchandise and property. Most of the younger, marriageable men were maimed or died in attempts to stop the seasonal attacks of the invaders from the eastern desert, or were captured and killed.

---

5.   Cf. Holland 1992.

6.   Mt. 1.5.

7.   Deut. 20.10-18; Josh. 6–7; cf. Rambam (Maimonides), *Kings* 6.4, for conditions and targets for demolishing, killing and banning. Also Niditch 1993, esp. the 'Conclusions' (150-55).

8.   Deut. 21.10-14.

9.   Dever 1992.

None of my brothers and sisters was ever taught how to earn a living outside the family firm which, in fact, was so well-established that while it lasted it nearly ran itself, sustaining all of us in the extended household.[10] Now we felt helpless. Our family compound, usually so joyful, became silent. Especially my mother, who has hitherto spent a lifetime of relative leisure (if you discount the fact that she was always pregnant; she gave birth to fourteen babies; six of whom survived beyond early childhood; this, given our usual infant mortality rates, was pretty good[11]). Our country relatives left their homes and came to ours, since all their property had been vandalized or taken over, and they feared for their lives. It was rumoured that the infiltrators/invaders were a cruel crowd; they took whatever they could: chattels, animals, food. They burned and destroyed whatever they couldn't take. They dressed like barbarians. Most of them were illiterate.[12] Their women and children were socially inferior to adult males, especially the elders. They had strange religious practices. But they were invincible, they pressed forward, behaving as if our ancient and civilized land belonged to them. So great was their self-conviction that our own people became scared and ran: we hadn't had war for decades, we have been so peacefully intent on our good life. We were urban and peaceful, rather gentle: we were nothing like our neighbours to the east of the Jordan, the Moabites who would sacrifice infants for the common interest.[13] Or like the traders from the north, our sea-faring cousins the Phoenicians. We didn't know how to fight back and how to react—first to their infiltration of our hinterland from the east, then to their continued presence.

On the other hand, these people's physiognomy and language were undeniably close to ours. Had we been a racially prejudiced society (as traders we could not afford to be), we would have said that they must have shared some ethnic pool with us. We were wondering how we could

10. For definitions and descriptions of late Bronze and Iron Age Israelite 'households' and 'families', rural and urban: Meyers 1997; Blenkinsopp 1997; Bendor 1994. It can be assumed that, perhaps more in urban than in rural areas, the structures of so-called Canaanite households did not differ that much from structures obtainable in so-called Israelite groups.

11. See Brenner 1997: 59-71.

12. On the spread of literacy in 'Ancient Israel', there is a widespread agreement among scholars that it could not have occurred before the eighth century BCE—as also supported by archaeological data.

13. 2 Kgs 3.26-27.

exploit the similarities in order to contain or repel them. But meanwhile, food was becoming very scarce. Commodities, international trade, communication came to an almost complete halt. My father's house, our kinship unit, could no longer function—as it should have, this was its *raison d'être*; we're not talking emotions here—as an economic unit successfully providing for its various consanguinous and other members.

I was just coming of age. I was quite well educated: in our family male and female siblings alike were literate. Our parents taught us at first; then we had tutors.[14] The women too knew about textiles, helped in the business. We were introduced in court; we had social connections. We had property, including real estate. But we had no food. And together with my sisters, older and younger, I could find nobody to marry: it became so bad that up to seven women would beseech a single man to marry them, for food and honour.[15] Gradually it dawned on me that the only way to gain some livelihood for me and for my family would be to open a brothel: such institutions flourish especially during hard times. With an eye to the changing situation, with the knowledge that ultimately the invaders would covet our walled city, with cold calculation, I asked my parents to have the lease of a house by the city wall. I was given a house from the family estate. I turned it into an organized, clean establishment. What can a woman do?[16] We had a nice byline in paid hospitality, food-selling too. In fact, some of the later Jewish commentators insist I was just that, a food-seller and an innkeeper.

This is nonsense, of course: prostitution, because of male cupidity, is a much more stable and viable occupation than even food-selling. That later generations attempted to emphasize my choice, or obliterate it, is beside the historical point.[17] In addition, we processed flax regularly, to help

14. For examples of schooling at home, see various passages in Prov. 1–9. For the issue of schooling, see, among others, Lang 1980.

15. Isa. 4.1.

16. For the by now classic analysis of prostitution in ancient Israel (again, there is no reason to believe that other indigenous populations had different social conceptions), see Bird 1989; also van der Toorn 1989.

17. So clearly in the Aramaic Targum to Josh. 2. This is also cited by Rashi and mentioned by Radak in his commentaries to Judg. 11.1 and 16.1, and by Ralbag in his commentary on 2 Kgs 3. Abrabanel takes a middle position between the two explanations, 'innkeeper' and 'whore': he states that (1) a woman's modesty is ultimately affected by the things she sees, the people she meets, etc., if she's an innkeeper; and (2) most female innkeepers had been prostitutes before starting the inn business. Josephus (*Ant.* 5.1.2) forgoes Raḥab's profession (which he never mentions) and

father, since all better textiles could not be sold by then. Men started to flock to my 'house', Raḥab's house, the 'Broad's house', from Jericho as well as from outside it (as long as the roads were open). In spite of my relatively young age, I was the madam. I ran the show. I shall leave aside the question of whether or not I supplied sexual services myself. At any rate, my girls were clean and discreet. Knowledge about abortifacients and birth control, officially denied but preserved as female oral traditions, was turned into praxis, thus preventing complications for girls and customers alike.[18] In short, my business flourished. I now knew everybody, and everybody knew me.[19] My family was now both shamed and ashamed,[20] but was also hungry no more. Situated as I was by the city gate and meeting (so to speak) many travellers and politicians and other eminent males, as well as ordinary people (I ran an egalitarian establishment; modest rates, value for money, few questions), my political awareness grew by the day. Through listening to many conversations I came to realize that those invaders, those 'Hebrews' as they called themselves, might prevail, might inherit the land. I began to realize this might indeed happen. Not so much because of their wit, neither because of their potent god (they only had one god, no goddess at all—hard to imagine at the time—or so they said), but because of our complacency, our blindness, our fat and peaceful ways. A scandal about the reinforcement of the city wall, not done properly by the appointed contractor, and corruption in the matter of hand-thrown defence stones[21] (communal warehouses found mysteriously half-empty), were unsettling. And I was uneasy in my heart.

Well, one day in the early summer two strangers came to my establishment. Their version of the story or, rather, the story as seen from their

---

designates her an innkeeper from beginning to end. For other, traditional Jewish possibilities of understanding the Heb. זונה, literally 'harlot' or 'prostitute', see *Sif. 'Emor* 1.7 (for Lev. 21.7). It seems, nevertheless, that the simpler reading is preferable to others, motivated by the ideological attempt of exonerating a future foremother from a shady past.

18. Brenner 1997: 72-89, for female knowledge and use of prevention and abortion agents in the ancient Near East, including Egypt and ancient Israel.

19. Cf. *B. Zeb.* 116b, as also in Rashi and *Yalqut Shimeoni*: 'There was no great man or high official in the land with whom Raḥab did not have intercourse.'

20. For oriental/Mediterranean concepts of female shame and male honour see Pilch 1997, with references to further secondary literature.

21. See Judg. 9 for the [Canaanite] woman who kills Abimelek by throwing a grindstone at him from a city wall. For stones as weapons, see also Yadin 1963: 232-33 [Hebrew]. Throwing stones are also mentioned in Ugaritic literature as 'hand stones'.

source group, is written in the book called after their chieftain, Joshua (ch. 2). I knew they were strangers right away. Local dress codes couldn't be applied; their language, though intelligible, sounded a bit quaint and antique. They weren't particularly clean. Their skin was rough. One pretended to be a travelling carpenter, the other a travelling potter.[22] But their act was not convincing. They were watchful, observant,[23] conversational. I had a hunch that they were spies for Joshua's small crowd: rumour had it that they were nearing the city anyway. They had done their best to run a propaganda campaign, trying to convince the city's king and council that their army was a huge 'national' army, that we should surrender without battle.[24] The king and his council laughed. So here were the spies, I thought.

But what kind of spies? Inadequate and comical, I would say.[25] They had no proper cover story: they did not speak the dialect of Gibeon, from where they claimed to originate. They referred to each other as 'brother',[26] but displayed no kin resemblance. They didn't look like travelling artisans. They didn't even step out for a walk, to inspect the city walls, for instance.[27] In fact the heat was unbearable and they didn't take advantage of the afternoon breeze to learn about their surroundings. They stayed put. They drank, a lot. They had their fun with the girls. They appreciated my food. They paid and tipped. Then they went to sleep, as if they were safe in their own territory. They seemed careless.[28] And yet—there was something forceful about them, somewhat menacing and aggressive yet at the same time curious and selfish. So I spied on them, and watched them. Discreetly.

---

22. For the spies' cover stories, a grand gap-filling, see Radak and *Yalqut Shimeoni*. The Hebrew word used for this gap-filling means, literally, 'quietly, secretly', as also translated in the Aramaic Targum; but is consonantly identical with a word meaning 'smith', 'artisan'. The motivation is of course an attempt to make the story seem more realistic.

23. Cf. Josephus, *Ant.* 5.1.2.

24. Cf. Rambam (Maimonides), *Kings* 6.5 (in paraphrase): Before he entered the land Joshua sent to them [the land's inhabitants] three messages. The first, whoever wants to flee should flee. The second, whoever wants to make peace should make peace. The third, whoever wants to make war...

25. See Zakovitch 1990.

26. As often in the Hebrew Bible, for instance in Lev. 25.

27. Which they in fact do in Josephus's version (*Ant.* 5.1.2).

28. Abrabanel notes in his commentary that the text hints at the spies' apparent misconduct and carelessness.

The king's men came towards evening, You're harbouring Hebrew
spies, they said; hand them over. Now, I'd never fully understand why I
denied any knowledge of them. The denial was instinctive: my motives,
for whatever they were worth, could be analysed later. At the time, they
were of no consequence. I reminded the captain of the guard, briskly, that
his wife could be told about his recent visits to my establishment. He
turned away together with his men, not searching the premises properly—
when notified of their arrival, I've quickly arranged to hide the Hebrew
'spies' on the roof, under some flax drying in preparation for its processing
by my girls. They were lying there, frightened and silent. They were in my
hands. I had to decide what to do.

By nightfall I've made my decision. I'll help them escape—on condition
that they promise me that, if they conquer the city, they will grant political
asylum to me and to the rest of my family. Please understand: their stories
present me as being full of faith in their eventual success, hanging on the
power of their omnipotent, single god. They even make me present a
speech to that effect (Josh. 2.9-13). The truth was different. Although at
the time I didn't really believe they'd ever manage to conquer the city, I
decided to let them go—if they gave me their word—as insurance against
a possible eventuality. I can hear you think, but that's treason in terms of
your source community. I can answer, ideals aside, I was beginning to
suspect that political and material survival were at stake. To all intents and
purposes, I was by then acting as the head of my father's house; the
responsibility hung heavily upon me. I was no convert[29] to the new
religion, a religion without goddesses. Presentations of me as such, for
instance in the Christian text called 'Letter to the Hebrews' (11.30-31),
make me chuckle to myself. I acted rather than 'believed' (Jas 2.25)
because I could act, because my vanity rejoiced in the possibility that I
could affect local history, because I too love to be childish and play spies,
because I love to defy authority (the king's, in this case). And the thrill of
danger! And the sense of revenge. I remembered the gossip about my
'house', the shaming—as in other eastern societies, shaming in ours had a
devastating effect, especially the shaming of women in the name of male
honour.[30] But, primarily, I did it because I wanted that extra insurance.

So I extracted a promise from the so-called spies. That indeed was a
richly humorous scene: I had them hanging on a rope, between heaven and

29. But according to the *Mekhilta*, she converted to Judaism after 40 years of
harlotry (during the wilderness period).

30. Bechtel 1991; Klein 1995.

earth, speaking at length and demanding an oath before letting them off on the outside of the city wall. Luckily I knew the schedule of the guards' patrols; luckily, I could give the spies directions for a temporary hideaway.

So you may ask, how sure were you that they'd keep a promise thus extracted under duress? I wasn't, actually. An oath is an oath, though.[31] And the whole thing was a long shot.

You know the rest of it, as told in Joshua 2 and 6. They managed to escape. They went back to Joshua. How they glossed over their behaviour, their inadequacy as spies, I don't know. They managed to convince their leader that all inhabitants of the land were convinced of their might. Later they managed to conquer Jericho—they say the walls were felled down by their god, after their priests circled it blowing their ritual trumpets. I was there, so can tell you how it really was. An earthquake, not big on the Richter scale, perhaps 4 or 5; but the walls haven't been maintained properly; and it was easy for the Israelites—this is how they started to call themselves rather than 'Hebrews', as soon as they began to annex territories here and there—to take it from there, in the panic that ensued. (If you press me I'd agree that the timing of earthquakes can be divinely determined, at least in theory. This would make the event a miracle by definition, by timing; but I am and always have been a sceptic, you see.) So they came, they saw, they conquered. And demolished the city and its civilization. And looted: whether they used the loot or sacrificed it as burnt offering to their god (such uncivilized and commercial waste!) is immaterial. And they killed. And they saved me and my father's house, all gathered in my house that was marked by a red ribbon. And they wrote everything down for posterity, including the ideo-religious embellishments, and a very serious attempt at saving face for the spies/agents of victory.

So my life and my family's life was saved. But otherwise… The business was lost. Everything was lost. My family dispersed: they were assimilated into the inferior culture of the conquistadors. It was easily done: similar origins, similar backgrounds, similar language. There was the little matter of official religion, monotheism they called it: you weren't supposed to worship any of the old deities but only one, Yhwh. This was in fact no problem since many traits of the old religion were incorporated in him; besides, even the Hebrews/Israelites weren't as strict about

31. Cf. the version of the story in this point in Josephus (*Ant.* 5.1.2): the spies' oath was rectified by Joshua, Elʻazar the high priest and the elders' council, hence was absolutely valid and secure.

worshipping only him for centuries to come, remonstrations by their spiritual leaders notwithstanding.[32]

And what happened to me? There's nothing about my eventual fate, beyond being saved, in the Israelites' first canon of holy writs. Later on, when they were already 'Jewish' and their sages were compiling subsequent tomes, some of them commentaries on and updates of the original writings, they noticed my disappearance from the earlier text and speculated about me. They had me domesticated, of course, made me into a wife and mother. I was made foremother of a linen-making family guild by virtue of my flax drying on the roof, in which I hid the spies. I was made into a foremother of priests and prophets, including Jeremiah and Huldah,[33] even foremother of kings.[34] They were prepared to forget—my foreignness, and forgive—my sexual past, my being a broad. The overriding consideration for them was that I acted out of faith.[35] At times they even had me converted, as I mentioned earlier in my story.[36] Baloney, as I've explained.

The Christians, to their credit, they married me off to a prominent figure. They put me straight into the lineage of king David and, therefore, their own Messiah, in one of their first canonized testimonies: 'Salmon [was] the father of Boaz by Raḥab, and Boaz the father of Obed by Ruth, and Obed the father of Jesse, and Jesse the father of King David' (Mt. 1.5-6). They also made me into a model of faith in god (Heb. 11.30-31) and action (Jas 2.25).

I'm not impressed, however, by all this good and—as they think in my case—posthumous propaganda. First they make fun of me by nicknaming me the Broad; then they have me believe in their superiority and their god; then they forget about me, only to domesticate me once more in the service of their ideologies. The Christians are no better than the Jews in this respect. And, throughout it all, I have the feeling that they have constructed me as an anonymous woman, a nicknamed whore, in order to emphasize my faith or whatever else they attribute to me. You see, in their culture women are considered politically inferior to men. They reason that, if even a whore could realize the result of the Israelites' infiltration into Canaan, then her menfolk should have been that acute. If a whore has

32. Cornelius 1997; Edelman 1995.
33. *Ruth R.* 2, *Sif. Num.* 68, *Zut. Lam.* 1, *Sif. Zut.* 10, *Pesik. Kah.* 13.
34. *Eliyahu Zut.* 22.
35. *B. Zeb.* 116a, *Sot.* 34a, *Sif. Deut.* For Deut. 11.25, *Sif. Zut.* 10, *Mekhilta.*
36. *B. Zeb.* 116b.

faith, anybody else should. In short, they used me. And then, after I've done my bit, pressed me back into the mould all their women share, that of wifery and motherhood.

But the truth of the matter is that I did *not* become a wife and mother. That is a much later fiction, attempts to honour me (in their eyes) for what wasn't mine. Like other figures of fiction whose fate isn't specified in their original stories, who don't get to die in those stories, I live forever. I am forever young, forever attractive, I don't have to get married and bear children, I don't have to talk, I can continue to be near my beloved Jericho and observe. Observe it, and observe history and the way it is constructed into identities.

I was there, therefore, when my beloved city was rebuilt at a great personal cost to the contractor (there was a divine curse to prevent the reconstruction).[37] I saw how Jericho redeveloped again, slowly and over hundreds of years, from an oasis and watering place for passing tradesmen into a civilized city. Herod the great built a palace there. Men were again playing backgammon under the palms in the city's main square; elegant ladies were chaperoned and carried about. And so on. And then decline again—I lose count of the years, and it doesn't really matter.

And now, of course, things are happening again in Jericho. Recently it was given to a political body that calls itself a Palestinian-state-to-be, or something like this. Most of these 'Palestinians' are Moslems, another religion yet. They claim to own the place, and other territories conquered by the Israelis a few years back. Now, the Jews suffered greatly before they came back to the land they took over, and not always gently, from us 'Canaanites': this is true. They are now back in their land, they have a political organization called a state. Since they trace their lineage to the Israelites/Hebrews that took the land from us, they lay claim to all of it. The Palestinians, on the other hand, also claim that it's theirs. (Their roots might be shorter than the Israelites', but they are long enough.) People are sitting again in the town squares, playing backgammon. Traders travel through it and cross the Jordan bridges. I look at my beloved city. Jericho is more of a village now. It will grow again, though. I wish that those squabbling descendants of the Israelites—if they are that—and descendants of Yishmaʻel—if they are that—would remember that this city has been there for thousands of years. It has outlived many rulers,

---

37   Josh. 6.26; The curse specified that the man who rebuilds the city would lose his firstborn upon laying the wall's foundations, his youngest upon completion. The realization of the curse is reported in 1 Kgs 16.34 (during King Aḥab's reign).

many governments. It has outlived the 'Canaanites', the 'Israelites', the Jews, the Romans, among others. It will outlive the present conflict between Israelis and Palestinians. It will flourish once more. My beloved city will return, only to be reconquered and retaken, demolished and rebuilt, inhabited and deserted.

I am Raḥab, the broad. Nobody knows my real name. I live, I see things: I'm in your holy texts. As long as they continue to serve as such, I'm alive and well. And so is my city, the ancient Jericho of the Asian–African great rift, by the Dead Sea.

I, DELILAH: A VICTIM OF INTERPRETATION

Yairah Amit

Am I a Philistine? A harlot? A traitor? Who is responsible for slandering my memory in history and for the role that Western culture has cast me in? What is my 'true' ancestry? Who am I? What are my feelings? What moved me to betray Samson to the Philistines? I shall try to answer these and other, equally important questions as we go on—and you, dear reader, try to hear me out without preconceived ideas.

I

The biblical editor devoted to me a narrative that today comprises 18 verses (Judg. 16.4-21). The reader of this story can only admit that its gaps make it impossible to determine my nationality, my social position, or generally my way of life. Indeed, as a reliable narrator he did not encumber you, the reader, with useless matter,[1] but his damnable reticence opened the door to numerous gap-fillings that scarcely flattered me.[2] On one point, however, the taciturn narrator did speak up, when he admitted that Samson loved me, but he was unwilling to put in even a word regarding my feelings for him—did I love him too, or was the relationship with him and his presence forced upon me? There is no question that the historical hostility to me has its roots here, because no one would forgive me for not loving Samson the judge, the hero, God's Nazarite. Before going on with my story, I had better explain what I mean by saying no one forgave me. I am referring to the commentators down the centuries—all of them men, of course, for no woman would have been formally allowed to engage in biblical interpretation, much less put it in writing. In any event, those commentators who were so impressed by the fact that Samson's love

---

1. On the reliability of the biblical narrator, see Amit 1992.
2. On the biblical narrative and its numerous gaps, see Perry and Sternberg 1968; Sternberg 1987: 186-229.

for me was mentioned explicitly, never asked if I cared for his company, or consented to it out of fear, duty and the like... As for me, my ego and feminine self-esteem make me happy that at least the biased author saw fit to record Samson's love for me right from the start (v. 4). As a skilled practitioner of the poetics of biblical narrative, this author does not waste words and does not give too much information about the feelings and thoughts of his characters.[3] Thus the fact that he noted them in my case gives me a special status among the other women in Samson's life. The Timnite woman is described as a daughter of the Philistines (Judg. 14.1-4); the Gazaite is described as a harlot, and because of her residence in Gaza, assumed to be a Philistine—as though the Gaza market had no whores from Egypt, Phoenicia and the like. The interpretative imagination is often limited, thus analogy is a favourite tool of these narrow-minded commentators. Although nothing was said about my origins, and although my habitation in the Valley of Wadi Ṣorek—rather than in one of the five cities of the Philistines: Gaza, Ashdod, Ashkelon, Gath and Ekron—should have made it difficult to define me as a Philistine, so strong is the inclination to do so, that despite the elements that suggest an Israelite identity, the scholars and the commentators alike tend to ignore them. A typical case is that of Joseph Naveh, author of the entry 'Wadi Ṣorek' in the Hebrew Biblical Encyclopedia.[4] He begins by noting the objective fact that this place is mentioned only in connection with me. Then he points to two facts which show that it was an Israelite settlement: (1) that it was near Zorah, which is known to have been an Israelite settlement in that period; (2) that the Hebrew name Ṣorek, which means 'goodly vine' (Isa. 5.2; Jer. 2.21; Gen. 49.11), suggests that it was a region of plentiful vineyards, without a hint of its being Philistine. Nevertheless, Naveh concludes the entry with the following statement:

> Assuming that the stories in Judg. 14 and 16 about Samson in Wadi Ṣorek and in Timnah have a common geographic background, it could be deduced that the name Nahal Ṣorek in Judg. 16.4 refers to the area of Timnah, that is, to the section of Wadi a-Ṣrar west of Zorah that was inhabited by Philistines in the time of Samson.

This final statement shows that the strong desire to place the story in a Philistine context has given rise to a tendentious geographic interpretation.

---

3.   For the fashioning of personae in the biblical narrative, see Gunkel 1901. But see also Sternberg 1987 and more recently Polak 1994: 255-301.

4.   See Naveh 1968.

To achieve this, Naveh was obliged to suggest that the Samson stories in chs. 14 and 16 have a common setting, and in referring to the brook that formed a natural boundary between the tribal lands of Dan and Judah, and to confine himself to the section near Timnah.[5] Here geography is enlisted to serve a common and popular interpretation that the scholar seems unable to shake off.

You may have noticed that the biblical account does not condemn me explicitly, even if it cannot be said that I am portrayed as a positive character. The analogy between me and the Timnite woman who betrayed Samson's riddle to her people, the Philistines, does not flatter me at all. On the contrary—in the case of the Timnite woman there were extenuating circumstances, as she was threatened that both she and her father's house would be set on fire (Judg. 14.15). There is also in her story a phrase that suggests a patriotic motive for her actions—she refers to the guests at the wedding feast as 'my people' (v. 16), and the narrator repeats it, stating in the conclusion that she told the riddle to her people (v. 17). This repetition on the narrator's part creates the effect of represented or combined speech, whereby the narrator expresses the Timnite woman's own feelings.[6] By contrast, there is no suggestion that I was ever threatened. Moreover, those commentators regard me as the embodiment of extreme wickedness, because I agreed to take money. The author employed the poetics of repetition to emphasize the issue of money, thus labelling me for all time as one who sold her soul to the devil. I shall not dwell at length on this matter, except with the regard to the author's reiteration, which various commentators pounced on with glee. The subject of money is first brought up by the lords of the Philistines: 'and we'll each give you eleven hundred shekels of silver' (16.5),[7] and at the end of my story it is said that 'the lords of the Philistines came up and brought the money with them' (v. 18).[8] In other words, it is not suggested that I was in any way

5.   See the list of tribal boundaries in the book of Joshua (15.10-11; 19.41-43). A main road from the coastal plain to Jerusalem passed through Wadi a-Ṣrar. According to Naveh, it was along that route that the ark was returned: 'The cows went straight ahead along the road to Beth-Shemesh' (1 Sam. 6.12).

6.   An examination of the theory of 'represented speech' or 'combined speech' is found in Even 1968 and Golomb 1968. More recently, see also Arpaly 1998: 285-313, and the bibliography supplied there.

7.   A comparison with the story of Micah (Judg. 17.3) serves to show the huge economic value of eleven hundred pieces of silver, yet in the present case it was five times as much.

8.   It appears that a haplography of *waw* occurred in the Hebrew text here.

threatened, nor are there any hints of tribal or national motivation. I am portrayed as being moved entirely by greed, as a person who wanted a lot of money, and having won it, becomes unforgivable.

II

A close look at the history of interpretation reveals that the uncertainty about my origins gave rise to diverse possibilities, some of them quite startling. So it is in the literature of the Sages. Significantly, those wise men, some of whom were notable for their creative imagination, their national solidarity, and their view of women as personifying all that is earthly and physical, did not describe me as a Philistine or as harlot.

The Mishnah tractate *Naz.* 1.2, devoted to the rules of the Nazarite, the definition of Samson's vows and the distinction between it and lifelong Nazarism, states: ' "I will be like Samson", "like the son of Manoah", "like the husband of Delilah", "like him that tore up the gates of Gaza", or "like him whose eyes the Philistines put out…" '.[9] I am referred to as Samson's legal spouse, with no suggestion that I was a stranger, an alien woman. This view is supported by a midrash, which states that 'her son Samson was killed by his wife, for it is said, He loved a woman in Wadi Ṣorek, whose name was Delilah'.[10]

Furthermore, Samson's association with me was not a pretext (Judg. 14.4), as it was with the Timnite and the Gazaite, whose relations with Samson led to massacres of Philistines. Indeed, his connection with me led to the opposite—his delivery into the hands of the Philistines and his death in captivity. Notwithstanding, these experts of analogy failed to note the difference between the cases, or that there was no reason to relate me to the Philistines. In other words, please keep in mind that both in the biblical narrative and in the Sages' writings, there is no 'foreign' or 'other' aspect to the relationship between me and Samson. The Bible does not call me a Philistine, and some of the Sages admit that I was a legal wife.

And that is not all. In a collection under the name *Midrashic Treasury*, which contains some stories ascribed to Eldad Hadani, there are actual references to the fruit of that marriage, namely, the sons who were born to Samson and me, whose existence is usually ignored: 'And there are among the heroes the offspring of Samson, sons of Delilah, who run forth to make

9.   Danby 1933: 281.
10. Buber 1902: 107.

war, and the smallest of these will pursue many of them...'[11]

Nevertheless, I have to admit that some of the Sages disapproved of my delivering Samson to the Philistines, and went out of their way to condemn me, yet their discourses never hint that I was a Philistine. The Gemara notes that whereas the former women in Samson's life remain anonymous—his mother, the Timnite, her sister and the harlot of Gaza—I am mentioned by my name. They grasped that this was no accident, and deduced from it, by a method of associative etymology that has no relation to reality and many know that it is both popular and lacking a scientific basis, that my name, Delilah, is a reference to my destructive role in his life. It was in the tractate *Soṭah* in the Babylonian Talmud (9.2) that my name was first interpreted pejoratively:

> Rabbi says: If her name had not been called Delilah, she was fit that it should be so called.[12] She weakened his strength, she weakened his heart, she weakened his actions. 'She weakened his strength', as it is written, 'And his strength went from him' (Judg. 16.19). 'She weakened his heart', as it is written, 'And when Delilah saw that he had told her all his heart' (v. 18). 'She weakened his actions' since the Shechinah departed from him, as it is written, 'But he wist not that the Lord had departed from him' (v. 20).[13]

Rabbi's explanation of my name was in line with the tradition of punning upon names in biblical literature. Thus my name was interpreted as hinting at my conduct and destiny: Delilah, because I weakened Samson, and it matters not that the verb *dldl* appears only in the Sages' literature and is probably post-biblical,[14] for as we know, respect for dia-chronical perception was not one of the Sages' virtues, and their dis-courses are rife with anachronisms.

The keen interest in my sexuality and passions, evinced by many male commentators, is also found in the Sages, revealed in their surprising interpretation of the phrasing used in the biblical narrative, specifically of the word *wate'alaṣēhu* (= 'forced him'),[15] which justifies its sequel: 'he was wearied to death' (v. 16). This pressure, as a result of which Samson

---

11. Eisenstein 1928: 20.

12. The Sages explain the name 'Delilah' from *dildel*, being a root form for a verb that means 'diluting' or 'weakening'.

13. See, e.g., the Babylonian Talmud (Epstein 1933: 43); *Num. R.* 9.24, etc.

14. See, e.g., *m. Neg.* 6.7; *m. Soṭ.* 9.15 etc.

15. A singular word, common in Aramaic. A literal interpretation equates the root *alṣ* with the term *heṣiqah*, meaning 'harassed', or 'pressured'. The word was used to intensify the sense of pressure Delilah put on Samson. Cf. Moore 1895: 357.

gave up his secret, is interpreted by them with regard to a woman who rebels against her husband declining to perform wifely services and responsible in this case to interrupted coitus:

> Said R. Yose bar Haninah 'As to her, since she is obligated to him for seven [sorts of labour], he deducts from her marriage settlement seven, while in his case, since he is obligated to her for three [acts of labour], he adds three to her contract.'

The Gemara explains it thus:

> It is in line with what R. Yohanan said, 'The anguish of a man is greater than that of a woman'. There is a pertinent verse of Scripture, 'And when she pressed him hard with her words day after day, and urged him', What is the meaning of 'and urged him'? Said R. Isaac bar Eleazar, 'She would pull herself out from under him'. 'His soul was vexed to death', but her soul was not vexed to death. And there are those who say that she found the necessary satisfaction with other men. All the more so that she desired sexual relations![16]

Who am I to dismiss a tenuous interpretation which the rabbis chose to accept? I leave it to the philologists. I wish only to draw your attention to the Sages' creative imagination and their way of thinking, which does not lack sensitivity to the female side and the needs of women. Some of them understood a woman's suffering, and they regarded me as a flesh-and-blood woman with desires and needs of her own, not a woman to be condemned, but Samson's wife, who was not a too-devoted spouse, but was neither a Philistine nor a harlot.

III

Who, then, was the first to disparage me in this way? I think I can safely state that it was none other than the greedy, luxury-loving traitor, Josephus Flavius, whose book *Jewish Antiquities* retold the biblical narrative thus:

> Howbeit he [Samson] was already transgressing the laws of his forefathers and debasing his own rule of life by imitation of foreign usages; and this proved the beginning of his disaster. For, being enamoured of a woman *who was a harlot among the Philistines, Dalala by name*, he consorted with her; and the presidents of the Philistines confederacy [*sic*] came and induced her by large promises to discover from Samson the secret of that strength... (5.306-13, my emphasis).

---

16. See *y. Ketubot* 5.8 (Neusner 1985: 192).

Curiously, this Joseph ben Matityahu, who preferred to be known by his Roman name of Josephus Flavius, who abandoned his people and joined the victorious Romans who spared him and provided him with comfortable conditions for writing, did not consider that I, Delilah, might have been an Israelite like him, who had her appropriate reasons to cooperate with the Romans of her days, namely, the Philistines. It is said that he who criticizes sees his own failings in others, so this similarity may be why Josephus unconsciously chose to describe me as a harlot, and if a woman of this type, then a Philistine one, because the opulent Roman culture—which was distantly related to the descendants of the island of Caphtor, who are the Cretan-descended Philistines[17]—was somewhat more liberal in its treatment of such women than was the halakhic Jewish society of the Second Temple period. Moreover, Josephus, in his role of apologist for his people,[18] may have preferred to remove the traitorous harlot from his own national camp to that of the Philistines.

The extent of my being the victim of vilification at Josephus's hand is seen in his depiction of the shaving off of Samson's hair. And since his writings have been widely read in the West, many Western people remember the scene the way he described it.[19] In the biblical account, at the appropriate moment I called for a man who shaved off Samson's hair, but Josephus wrote: 'She reft him of his locks and delivered him to his enemies.' He makes no mention of the man, and the blame is thus entirely mine.[20] Thereafter the artists who depicted this scene invariably showed me shaving off Samson's hair. I am not trying to shirk my responsibility, but the appearance of that 'man' is not fortuitous, because I was only the tool, and the question must be asked, who was behind me—the Philistines? Or also Israelites?

In any event, Josephus's attitude to me is most obvious in his concluding words about the life of Samson: 'That he let himself be ensnared by a woman must be imputed to human nature which succumbs to sins'

17. For Caphtor as linked to the Philistines, see Amos 9.7; Jer. 47.4. For the connection between Caphtor and Crete, see Ezek. 25.16; Zeph. 2.5.

18. See Josephus, *Against Apion*.

19. See Tümpel 1993: 155-67.

20. The Masoretic text has *wategalēaḥ,* suggesting she rather than the man shaved off Samson's hair, but it leaves the man without a clear role in the scene, and modern commentators have proposed to read *wayegalēaḥ,* meaning that the man did it.

(*Ant.* 5.317).[21] This statement also tells us about his general view of women, but that is another matter.

IV

A meticulous and exact interpretation that steers close to the text and abstains itself from filling gaps would have avoided classifying me as a Philistine or as a harlot. And, indeed, so did Jacob Liver, an honourable man, who wrote:

> But there is no evidence that she was a Philistine. The image of the unbeatable hero who reveals his secret to his beloved, and she betrays him and delivers him to his enemies, may be found in the legends of many nations.[22]

At long last, in Liver's description, I am shown as the person who appears in the Bible: a woman who was loved, about whom there is no evidence that she was a Philistine. Liver finds the answer to the question, why I betrayed Samson, in the treasury of quasi-realistic literary motives which abound in legends—and legends, as we know, allude, more or less explicitly, to the real world. Thus Liver, like the Sages, avoids defining nationality and occupation, and his interpretation leaves open the possibility that I was always a part of my Israelite people.[23]

V

But most commentators adopted Josephus's interpretation rather than that of the Sages. They described me as a Philistine, though many were kind enough to avoid associating me with the oldest profession in the world. Here is a handful of examples, taken from a vast collection which it would be wearisome to list.

According to G.F. Moore: 'Samson again falls in love with a Philistine

21. According to Ps.-Philo 43.5-6 (see Charlesworth 1985: 357), Delilah was a Philistine harlot whom Samson married.

22. See Liver 1965: 656.

23. Boling (1975), for example, follows Liver's cautious approach and does not mention Delilah's nationality. Likewise, the Hebrew poet Leah Goldberg, in her poem 'The Love of Samson' (Goldberg 1973: 228-32) also remains faithful to the biblical text and stops short of making Delilah a foreigner. The concluding line in the poem—'And her friends put out his eyes'—does not necessarily mean that she was a Philistine. But the poet does emphasize the love aspect and the destructive relationship, which meant that Samson was unable to leave Delilah though he knew she betrayed him.

woman.'[24] Likewise Elitzur is certain that I was a Philistine.[25] Burney is careful not to depict me unequivocally as a Philistine, and while vacillating between that and an Israelite, though inclined to the former, he proposes another possibility which—as we shall see—would be picked up by others:

> We are not told whether the woman was a Philistine, or an Israelite in the pay of the Philistines, though the general trend of Samson's inclinations favors the former supposition. Her name is Semitic in *form*, but this affords no indication as to her nationality, since Semitic names appear to have been largely used among the Philistines...[26]

Further down he refers to me as Samson's 'paramour'.

Burney, then, cast me as a Philistine lover, but he went further and by an unexpected flourish made me once more a harlot, though of a higher quality, namely, a temple prostitute. The etymological examination of the name Delilah leads him to discover an Akkadian influence on the story:

> Comparison with the Bab. proper names *Dalil-(ilu)-Ištar, Dilil-(ilu)-Ištar*, 'worshipper of *Ištar*'...the connotation of this name (at least according to the original form of the tale) can hardly be mistaken, Delilah must have been a sacred prostitute devoted to the service of the goddess.[27]

Burney also notes the resemblance between the biblical story about Samson and me and the tale of Enkidu and the harlot in the Epic of Gilgamesh. He describes Samson as Enkidu, whose strength was supernatural, and who was lost when he consummated his love with a woman. He finds another parallel in Greek mythology, and notes that Hera's hostility was the primary cause of the afflictions of Heracles—thus giving me a mythological status. Analogy is a highly flexible method, and there are almost unlimited similarities to be drawn between any two subjects, and in difficult cases the analogy may be drawn by contrast. Thus, it seems to me that while Samson may have some features in common with Enkidu, the man of the earth, or likewise Hera and I,

---

24. Moore 1895: 351.

25. See Elitzur 1976: 150.

26. Burney 1970: 377.

27. Burney 1970: 407; Noth (1966: 227) proposes interpreting the name Delilah as cognate with the root *dll/dlh* (cf. Cant. 7.6), meaning 'with long hanging locks'. See also the interpretation in Zakovitch (1982: 182-83), who finds similarities between the Song of Songs and the story of Samson, and interprets the name 'Delilah' as 'locks of hair', and argues that this is a midrashic name derivation based on a synonym, meaning, in this case, a weave, a plait or a loom.

nevertheless, the differences in these cases are greater than the similarities.

Soggin follows Burney in ascribing a theophoric value to my name, while suggesting that I might have been a Canaanite. Aware that there is no textual basis for this supposition, he adds that, judging by Samson's inclinations, as they appear in the narrative, it is also possible that I was a Philistine. The fact that my name bears some resemblance to that of the demoness Lilith suggests another idea to him, namely, that this was a deliberate attempt to disparage me by hinting at her name.[28]

Zakovitch also suggests that the seductress's nationality was deliberately left out, to blacken her character. According to him, the Timnite's betrayal of Samson's secret was understandable, arising as it did from patriotism and fear—thus I am worse than she. But using the Timnite to vilify me is only one side of the medal—the Israelite side. According to Zakovitch, behind the Israelite story lies a Philistine tradition, from which it was adapted.

Obviously, all assumptions about the prehistory of the biblical stories must be largely speculative—which is why scholarship demands evidence. To prove that this is in fact a Philistine tradition, Zakovitch proceeds in the direction indicated by Liver and shows that the story has parallels, suggesting that this is a common narrative motif: Jael who killed Sisera (Judg. 4.17-21; 5.24-27); Esther who defeated Haman (The Book of Esther, and particularly 7.8); and Judith and Holofernes (Judith 3–13).[29] Yet the common denominator in these stories is the depiction of a woman as a national heroine, quite unlike my case. Zakovitch explains the discrepancy between the expected use of the motif and the actual story as an indication that it originated as a Philistine tradition, in which the motif functioned as expected and I starred as the national heroine, and that the story was distorted in process of converting it into an Israelite one. According to this analysis, I was originally a national heroine of the Philistine nation, and the hostile Israelite narrative deprived me of my heroic stature and cast me in the role of a greedy seductress. Comparison with the parallel narratives led Zakovitch to note the lack of another motif in my story, namely, the erotic one. This is highly developed in the story of Judith (12.12, 16); hinted at in the king's suspicion of Haman and the charge he laid against him in Esther (7.8); and exegetes have also found it in the Song of Deborah in phrasing: 'At her feet he bowed, he fell, he lay down…' (Judg. 5.27), which the Sages also interpreted as meaning coition

28. Soggin 1981: 253.
29. Zakovitch 1982: 194-97.

(*m. Yeb.* 103.1; *m. Hor.* 10.2; *m. Naz.* 23.2). But Zakovitch explains that the suppression of the erotic motif had to do with the poetics of biblical narrative, and with respect for the context of the story. It is therefore not surprising that the erotic motif, deemed inappropriate for the biblical frame of reference, should crop up elsewhere, as in the writings of the Sages, and be given pride of place by diverse creative artists, who often found it a source of inspiration.

VI

You will have to forgive me for the didactic opening of this chapter, but prolonged dealing with commentators down the ages has taught me that this is an important matter. In the first place, it is a primary rule that an artistic work based on a character drawn from a familiar textual tradition, if it seeks to retain its link with the original work in order to give the new one added depth, must show some loyalty to the tradition on which it rests. The link enables the reader, or viewer, to recall the original, so that it may serve as the basis for comparison and for the appreciation of the singular new work. Therefore, an artist who wishes to make use of my character must be in some degree loyal to the biblical story, if only to the basic identities of the personae and the situation. This still leaves the artist considerable leeway to express his or her personal conception. The nature of the biblical story, which is verbal text, linear, generally laconic and with few external descriptions, leaves many gaps that may be filled in. No wonder then that creative people in diverse arts who used my image and sought to make it speak to their intended audience, took all kinds of liberties with it.[30] Some adapted me to their period and ambience, or to the artistic norms and messages of their time—so that I appear nude or clothed (as painted by Rubens), or as a Parisian prostitute (by Gustave Moreau), or as the epitome of the Orient in the imagination of a twentieth-century American (Cecil B. de Mille). Here a poet (John Milton) used my character to give vent to his personal preoccupations, and there I was employed for didactic or ideological purposes as a negative example. I feel flattered by this variety of approaches, delighted to have stirred the imagination of so many artists, but on the other hand, I am often angered by their one-sidedness, their obsession with the scene in which Samson's eyes are put out, and when they adapt me to fit Christian contexts, which

---

30. For a brief study of Delilah's figure in various artistic fields (painting, literature, opera and cinema), see Fishelov 1996.

are not really to my taste. But one cannot have everything, and this is the price I must pay for my bit of eternity in the museums and galleries that contain the best of Western civilization.

As far back as the thirteenth century I appeared as an illustration for Old Testament stories in the Christian Bibles, in which Samson and I were given a typological significance: Samson stands for Jesus and I stand for the Church. His love for me is therefore the Saviour's love for his Church. In this way I, Delilah of the wadi Ṣorek, came to serve a didactic purpose in the service of faith. The relationship between me and Samson matched the attitude of the Church towards the sensual pleasures, as spelled out by St Paul: '…it is good for a man not to touch a woman. Nevertheless, to avoid fornication, let every man have his own wife and let every woman have her own husband' (1 Cor. 7.1). I came to personify the danger of intimacy with a woman, who symbolizes sin, and as we have seen, it was Josephus who first proposed this direction of interpretation. You may evaluate my argument by looking at the artists of the renaissance, of whom the most prominent in this matter is Petrarch, the founder of Humanism. In his allegory *The Triumph of Love*, he names Samson the mightiest of men as one of love's victims—of course, because of me. Nevertheless, it could not be denied that as a woman I had something in common with Mary, the mother of Jesus, and might also represent a positive quality such as motherhood. This combination of good and evil, of motherhood and temptation, became a central feature of my personifications in Christian art.[31]

The Protestant Reformation made me an object of interest, since it legitimized the painting of biblical subjects that could be given a didactic significance. In the seventeenth century I kindled the imagination of a number of artists who used me as a warning against the seductiveness of sin.[32]

The Flemish artist Rubens (1577–1640), who painted many scenes from the Old and New Testaments, being faithful to the Christian tradition which viewed Samson as a forerunner of Jesus, and having enjoyed favourable experiences with whores, treated me sympathetically, showing me as a harlot who is also maternal. The composition shows Samson lying on my lap, my hand resting gently on his back while I gaze at him with tenderness,[33] the focus of the painting being my bosom, and the whole

31. Kahr 1972: 282-84. This thorough study covers the images of Delilah in Western art between the thirteenth and seventeenth centuries.

32. See Tümpel *et al.* 1991, 1993.

33. The composition of Rubens's painting, which belongs in the Frau Margret Köser Collection, Hamburg, suggests the traditional motif of the Pietà.

expresses both eroticism and motherhood, the latter quality being reiterated by the statue of Venus, the love goddess, and her child Cupid in the background. Yet my profession is made explicit by the presence of an old bawd at my side. In this way Rubens depicts me as simultaneously whorish and motherly.

The artist Van Dyck, who was influenced by Rubens, has shaped me extending my arms as though unwilling to part. His painting also evinces sympathy for me, despite the fateful consequences of the scene.[34]

Rembrandt (1609–69), who loved mythological, biblical and historical themes, painted a series of pictures on the subject of Samson during his marriage with his first wife, Saskia, believed to have been the model for Delilah in the paintings. Was this an expression of sympathy, or criticism? Or was it merely a pragmatic consideration?[35] I am certainly unable to answer this question, but his preferred composition makes me seem evil, which annoys me. He chose to depict me witnessing the blinding of Samson, retreating with his shaven locks of hair in my hands and gazing at the scene with no sorrow or horror on my face.[36]

John Milton, the seventeenth-century English poet (1608–74), in his dramatic poem *Samson Agonistes* (1671), also identified with Samson's tragedy.[37] He found common elements between his own unhappy fate and that of the biblical hero, whom he regarded primarily as a tragic figure. The similarities lay in the blindness, the sense of national mission, and the suffering caused by a woman's betrayal. Therefore to him I am first and foremost Samson's wife who hurt him, a Philistine who betrayed her husband for the sake of her people, expecting to win the glory enjoyed by Jael, the wife of Heber the Kenite, who killed Sisera. Though Milton describes me as Samson's wife, and therefore scarcely a harlot, yet my characterization as a false wife in a Puritan society accustomed for untold generations to equate the deceiving wife with the whore, taints me with harlotry.[38]

If Milton's personal experience dictated his imagination—and I am truly

---

34. Van Dyck's painting is in the Kunsthistorisches Museum, Vienna.

35. Kahr 1973. See also Fishelov 1996; these scholars claim that the choice of Delilah suggests the painter's ambivalent feeling for Saskia.

36. According to Fishelov (1996), she is fascinated by Samson's symbolic castration.

37. John Milton, *Samson Agonistes* (Collins 1950).

38. The biblical tradition that stresses faithfulness to God equates personal betrayal with whoring. This is evident in the prophets of the eighth century BCE, most notably Hos. 2–3, and likewise in the Deuteronomistic literature that was influenced by them.

sorry for him—two hundred years later the theme was taken up by Vladimir (Ze'ev) Jabotinsky (1880–1940), a Zionist leader and journalist who also wrote poetry and fiction, and in 1927 wrote the novel *Samson* in Russian.[39] He used it not only for the adventure of enriching the Hebrew literature with historical novels but also to express the conflict of an extreme national Zionist in front of a foreign developed world in the early decades of the twentieth century, so that the relations between Arabs, Jews and Englishmen form the background to the story of Samson and me. His Philistines are shown as a foreign nation with a highly developed conquerors' culture, full of charm but alien, deriving its vitality from ancient Crete and Troy. On the one hand, Samson respects the Philistine culture, with its tradition of administrative government and an organizational capacity for ruling over other peoples, as well as a sophisticated lifestyle, while on the other hand he is loyal to his tribe and his nation and is impelled to free them from Philistine domination. In depicting Samson's character in this way, Jabotinsky expressed his own ambivalent feeling about the British rule in Palestine over two nations, the Arabs, who are shown in the novel as the native Canaanite populace which serves the English/Philistine conquerors, and the Jews, represented by the Israelite tribes. The Israelites are fragmented, lack leadership and iron weapons, which makes it easier for the English/Philistines to dominate them. Samson/Jabotinsky seeks to drive out the conqueror, and urges his people to acquire iron, namely, weapons.

It is against this background that I am depicted as a green-eyed harlot, with an aroma of alien culture. Accordingly to Jabotinsky I had good reasons not to love the Philistines, because I was not really a Philistine, my mother having been a humble, downtrodden Avite concubine. I was deeply jealous of my older sister, Semadar, the Timnite, who was a pure Philistine and Samson's great love (Judg. 14). Moreover, I was gang-raped by Philistines when my father's house was burnt down (ch. 15). After this event, I spent several years in Thebes and Memphis, then came to Gaza, and was in fact the harlot with whom Samson lay when the Philistines sought to capture him, before he escaped from the city and carried away its gate (16.1-3). Samson did not recognize me as Semadar's sister. Once I moved to the valley of Ṣorek, he trusted me, because I had saved him from the Philistine ambush, and moreover, the praises of his boon companions made me something of a challenge for him. Jabotinsky's gap-filling has

---

39. The Hebrew translation by Baruch Krupnik (Karu) was first published in 1929 (Jabotinsky 1930).

me betraying Samson because of my deep psychological motivation. I could not accept that his only and one great love was my sister Semadar, the wife of his youth. My jealousy, according to this novel, had turned into infernal hatred. That is why I did not wish him to die, but to suffer lifelong humiliation. Seeking a psychological motive for my conduct, he still criticizes me, charges me with greed and condemns me to die in the Dagon temple with the other Philistines. After all, for him I was also a dangerous alien.

Cecil B. de Mille, the Hollywood producer, was inspired by Jabotinsky's novel to depict me as the jealous, rejected sister, consumed by a strong inferiority complex.[40] I betrayed Samson mainly because I was rejected by him. I was jealous not only of my sister Semadar (the Timnite wife), whom Samson loved, but also of Miriam, a Hebrew woman who loved him and tried to bring him back to his people. Thus de Mille strengthens the audience's sympathy with my character—in his film I always loved and never stopped loving Samson. He included a romantic scene in which I visit Samson in prison and offer to lay my life down to atone for my sin, telling him to kill me. I pray for his strength to return, so that we could flee to Egypt together and continue our love. Indeed, it is I who lead the blind Samson to the temple pillars, and not the lad mentioned in the biblical narrative. In this fashion I was neatly adapted to American morality and turned into a pious martyr, since I remained in the temple in order to die with Samson. Thanks to de Mille, I became a heroine of a romantic melodrama and a personification of the power of love.

So far we have seen that creative interpretation has infrequently depicted me in a positive light, though most often as a symbol of evil. The diverse interpreters have felt free to utilize my image to suit their personalities, their needs and circumstances of writing. I am especially distressed by being vilified in the minds of young children. The study of Mieke Bal, who analysed Dutch Bibles for children, showed that they are taught to regard me as a personification of feminine wickedness.[41]

David Fishelov's article poses the following question: 'Why did some artists "exonerate" Delilah, others judged her in keeping with the biblical text, while still others went out of their way to condemn her even more severely than the Bible?' He then proceeds to dismiss, one by one, feminist, biographical, religious and political arguments, and declares:

40. Forshey 1992: 60.
41. Bal 1987: 38.

Each of the above explanations illuminates a part of the truth, and even that only partially and inconclusively. But there is another explanatory direction, which seems to me more comprehensive and satisfactory than all the others: an artist whose main aim is ideological and didactic—assuming, for the sake of argument, that religion can be classified as an ideology—would tend to depict Delilah as a symbol of evil; another, who is chiefly concerned with the human dimension of the love story of Samson and Delilah, would be inclined to extenuate her case.[42]

I am not convinced that a single explanatory direction will provide the answer. My long experience shows that it is often difficult to separate ideology from the human dimension.[43] However, I hope that the survey of interpretations and their authors has persuaded you that I have been their victim. The time has now come to tell my 'true' life story.

VII

I am Delilah of the tribe of Judah. I always had a practical, strong-minded personality, which was why my father, who owned vineyards in the valley of wadi Ṣorek, on the border between Judah and Dan, sent me there to oversee the harvest.[44] There I first met Samson who used to wander in the vineyards. Samson fell in love with me and wanted to marry me. I never loved Samson, and married him only because my family and tribe pressed me to do so. They regarded the marriage as a way of discovering the source of his strength, in order to deliver him to the Philistines. The conflict between him and the tribe of Judah is well-known from the cycle of Samson stories. The Judaeans believed that the Philistines were threatening them because of Samson's raids, which no sensible person regarded as a war of liberation, and believed that once the Philistines laid their hands on him, they would let up on their tribe. We know that the injured Samson, having set fire to the fields of the Philistines and trounced them thoroughly, went and dwelt in the cave of the rock of Etam, in the territory of Judah (1 Chron. 11.6). In response, the Philistine armies came and camped in Judah. Needless to say, the tribal elders paid dearly for this

42. Fishelov 1996: 63.

43. The problem with this distinction would be shown by an attempt to classify Mieke Bal's study (1987), which tends to extenuate Delilah's act—and the reader would also have to decide if it is a feminist, ideological or human-aspect study.

44. For Delilah as an independent woman who is referred to by her own name and lives alone, see Bal 1987: 51. Bal also stresses that Delilah was not a harlot; she does, however, accept the common interpretation that she was a Philistine.

encampment. In any event, Samson knew that the Judaeans detested him, and that not only were they eager to turn him over to the Philistines, but were capable of killing him themselves. Therefore before surrendering to them he stipulated, 'Swear to me that you yourselves will not attack me' (Judg. 15.12). After the events in Gaza, when he had carried the gates of that city to the region of Hebron, also in the land of Judah, the Judaeans feared that the Philistines would wreak vengeance upon them. That was when my family and the leaders of the tribe urged me to marry Samson and discover the source of his strength, after which they would turn him in. At the same time, the Philistines also offered me a large sum of money if I delivered him into their hands. My people's experience had taught me that when Samson was bound with 'two new ropes' (v. 13), he could break free as though they were 'flax that catches fire' (v. 14), so when I asked Samson, 'what makes you so strong, and how could you be tied up and made helpless?' (16.6), and he responded with similar suggestions— 'seven fresh tendons' (vv. 7-9), or an unknown number of 'new ropes that had never been used' (vv. 11-12)—I knew he was lying. I, on the other hand, did not lie—I stated plainly time and again that I wished to know how to bind him so that he may become helpless.

Gradually my questioning turned into actual harassment. I made it plain to him that if he did not tell me his secret I would not remain with him. Discovering his secret became an obsession with me, and I had to find out whom Samson loved more dearly—me or his secret. I did not let him touch me, which was not difficult since I did not love him, and so he gave in. I delivered him to the Philistines. The man of Judah who was in the room helped me to do everything, and then took the 5500 pieces of silver that I had got from the Philistines to help our tribe recover from the depredations that Samson had caused. I am neither a Philistine nor a harlot, nor did I betray Samson—he knew that just as I had bound him, so I would cut off his hair.[45] I did this for the greater good of helping the people of my tribe, who were being ruled by the Philistines (15.11), while Samson revealed his secret because he wished to die—he was weary of his life's pretext (14.4) and of the strange fate of killing Philistines by means of women, yet never returning victorious from the field of battle.

I should have been praised like Jael, 'most blessed of women in tents' (Judg. 5.24). In those days my tribe did regard me as a national heroine.

45. Compare Bal 1987: 58-63. In her analysis, which includes psychoanalysis, Samson wished to be reborn because of his impotence, and Delilah served as his instrument to achieve this.

The question remains, why is Jael praised in the biblical literature, but not I? The answer is simple, that Jael belonged to the Kenite clan which joined the Israelites. I, on the other hand, was a daughter of the tribe of Judah who betrayed an Israelite judge who had gravely injured my tribe. This complex situation meant that my image would be ambivalent—neither a Philistine nor a harlot, but the woman who betrayed Samson. The Judaean editors suppressed my origins, because they did not want the tribe of Judah to be remembered in history as responsible for surrendering, and indirectly causing the death of an Israelite judge. At least those Sages who understood this described me as Samson's wife, the mother of his children. Josephus and the Christian interpretation disparaged me far more, he by depicting me as a Philistine harlot, they by choosing to depict Samson as forerunner of Jesus, adopting Josephus' view and casting me as a forerunner of Judas Iscariot and the sinful women among the disciples of Jesus. I could have forgiven them if, after describing me as a Philistine harlot, they had added me to the company of strong, independent non-Israelite women who took control of their destiny: Tamar, who disguised herself as a harlot; Raḥab, whose profession it was; Ruth, who paid a nocturnal visit to Boaz's threshing-floor; and the wife of Uriah the Hittite, who intentionally bathed in view of the king's roof. I would thus have become a link in the messianic chain. But it would seem that even the apostle Matthew knew that I was neither a foreigner nor a harlot, and left me out of the genealogy at the beginning of the New Testament (Mt. 1.1-17), where the mentioned women are foreign: Tamar, Rahab, Ruth and the wife of Uriah.

It remains for me only to return to my opening question and then sum up: I, Delilah, who sacrificed my private life to save my people, the tribe of Judah, have been a victim of interpretations.

JEZEBEL[*]

Hugh S. Pyper

So I am to tell my story now, is that it? Very good. And what am I? A name. In another story, long ago, all but my skull, the soles of my feet and the palms of my hands were food for dogs—war trophies, to be hung up. The rest of me was dung, so Jehu said, quoting Elijah, scattered and spread '…so none could say "This is Jezebel"'.[1] Well, prophet of Yhwh, if that is true, what is my task now? Who could say, even when I lived, in yet another story, 'This is Jezebel?' Which of you can say, 'This is I' of yourself, come to that?

If I must try, then it seems I must gather more than my wits, eh prophet? And where are you? Taken up in fire and whirlwind, they say, while I am earth. Earth to earth, ashes to ashes; even your own books consign me to no less than the common lot. And yet you readers know my name. My father and his sons, my mother, all his court, the teeming city where I grew up and laughed and danced, are nothing now while I…am a name. More than a name, a noun. Look me up: 'Jezebel: Name of the infamous wife of

*   In writing this paper, I am heavily indebted to and grateful for the work of Janet Howe Gaines whose recent book (Gaines 1999) is an unmatched study of the development of the Jezebel myth, beginning with a detailed reading of the biblical and other evidence and then moving on to a fascinating survey of high and low literature in English which has built up the picture of Jezebel the archetypal manipulative seductress. The reader is also referred there for an extended bibliography. I was privileged to be able to see a copy of this work in proof stage for which I record my thanks, both to the author and to the Southern Illinois University Press for their help and interest. I have also drawn heavily on Katzenstein (1997) for the historical reconstruction of Tyrian history, though aware that many of his reconstructions are inevitably conjectural. It should also be noted that the queen's version of events, fascinating as it is, is far from unbiased and may at times be speculative. I have tried respectfully to indicate the points where this might be the case.

1.   1 Kgs 9.36-37.

Ahab, king of Israel (1 Kgs 16.31 etc.); hence, a wicked abandoned woman, or a woman who paints her face'.[2]

How I admire that 'hence'! A world of prejudice in a word! Say my name. It tastes bitter-sweet, does it not, oozing juices at the start, moving through the buzzing languor of a flyblown afternoon to the tinkling tolling of that 'bel'—the belle of Baal's balls, perhaps? What is that taste? Something between disgust and desire, I fancy. Jezebel. Though you do not know who I am, you remember me, and knit my fertile members up into new women, paraded, parodied, as monstrous demonstrations of a female death. I lie on your tongue, something between Madame Ceauşescu and Evita, Bette Davis in a crimson dress.

See what I know now! And who is this you have given me this time to speak my words, to trap what I am in ink? A man, of sorts, sitting in a book-lined room, unanswered letters and student papers on his desk, tapping away at a keyboard, rearranging electrons on a screen; three thousand years, three thousand of your miles, or thereabouts, between us. My only chance to speak is in another language, another world, through another's hand. Some things do not change. When I spoke first, it too was through another's hand, a man's, I suppose, and of a different world, when Hebrew scribes wrote me into their tale of petty kings and paltry prophets, shaping me through their desire and their disgust. Then too I was tied down in alien words, a Gulliver in Lilliputian bonds of propaganda, a giant shipwrecked in Elijah's story, so it seems. Then, at least there were no footnotes, but let the Lilliputians tie me down, if they think it makes me manageable.

Remember, the tale says I know something of the power of writing too—sending a note to those pompous fools in Naboth's village, which scared them witless: writing under a man's power.[3] The king's seal on the tablet drained their self-righteous faces of colour and they lied. They knew where to find worthless fellows alright, that sort always do, seated in insufferable judgment in the dust, squatting in the gate of their collection of hovels. Not what is written, but the name in which it is written, does the trick, and though the seal was the king's they knew enough to send the reply to me.

And who taught them writing? Who was it but my people, who took the gift of writing from the hands of priests and scribes with their arcane scripts and years of training and their monopoly on what was written. You

---

who read me, in print on paper, or upon a screen, know it was my people who gave you these letters. My name is written on a seal as old as I am, which still you can read.[4] Who knows better than I, however, how letters can betray? 'E–zebel'—where is the exalted one?—my name, which foul-minded commentators turn to 'E–zebul'—where is the dung? What is written twists upon us, that I know too well. Beware then what you write of me, and what you read.

There's something Jehu learned! He sent a note to the cowards who were in Samaria, inviting them to do their duty and set up one of my husband's sons as king. Jehu, that upstart nobody, that king-killer! He was a bold man, I grant him that, and those dogs knew the voice of a master and turned on my children and my stepsons. Seventy of them he slew, the young lion turning on the cubs of his defeated rival. The gods curse him and his house! Had I his children in my grasp, I would do the same and more, I tell you!

Jehu makes it too into your dictionary: 'a: a fast or furious driver. b: a driver; a coachman. Hence as *vb.*, to drive furiously'.[5] Strange; where is 'Name of the notorious traitor and regicide of 2 Kings 9; *hence* a man who is a ruthless and treacherous usurper'? Unlike him, I am not accorded the accolade of action, of a verb, it seems. How would it be 'to jezebel', or indeed, 'to be jezebelled'? Naboth was, and Elijah, oh so nearly. Ahab knew what it was too, in other senses, and seldom complained.

Naboth?—a man out of place. Innocent? A man who defies his king is *innocent*? And what was his so-called claim that sent my royal husband sulking to bed like a spoilt child deprived of his toy? His ancestral rights. What ancestors? I ask. He dares mention ancestors? A man who, like all his kind, makes a virtue of being slave-born, who traces himself back to a starving rabble who fell on the towns of their betters and took them by sword. The gods save me from their wearisome recitations of this story which self-respect should long have silenced, a story sordid in itself, and patently untrue. An incredible people: even their own lies degrade them. A million dusty, starving desert raiders with their brats, so they say, fell on

---

4. Her Majesty is referring to a seal of unknown provenance, but of Phoenician style and dating from the eighth or ninth century BCE, which appears to have been overwritten with the letters *yzbl*. No relationship between the seal and the queen can be demonstrated, of course, but it is at least evidence that the name she bore, albeit in a non-biblical spelling, has been preserved from her time until now through the Phoenician invention of alphabetic writing (Gaines 1999: 60-61; Avigad 1964).

5. Onions 1973: 1129.

our cities and put us all to the sword. They tell us to our faces that our
forebears were wiped out—how can you answer such blind arrogance
except with scorn! Their impotent hatred can only wreak its murder on our
dead. Living, they know that we outmatch them. They never conquered us.
A few poor hill towns maybe they pillaged, but mostly they begged and
slaved and bought and sold to get what they could. If you believe their
tale, their father bought the land as a woman's grave. Naboth's fathers!
Impious too—the land has its Baal, its master and that master gives it to
the king.

Whoever his so-called ancestors were, and whoever their list of bandit
heroes snatching at kingship, none of them were men to match my father
Ethbaal, a man who wrested back the throne of Hiram from those bastard
upstarts who killed Hiram's son Abdastratus.[6] A nurse's whelps, indeed!
Not content to share the honour that their mother's breast was sustenance
for kings, they wanted all for themselves and killed the rightful king.
Tyrants as all the petty are when they gain power, their vision was too
small to do more than squat on the city and bleed it for what they could,
squabbling among themselves, like puppies fighting for a bitch's dugs.
Such was their greed that brother killed brother in the end, when Phelles
murdered Asthrymus to gain the throne.

But true blood will out and true faithfulness. My father, priest of Astarte
and scion of Hiram's house,[7] knew his time and struck without mercy in
the goddess's name, killing Phelles and gaining the city to popular
acclaim. At once he set about making its name and the name of its gods
revered throughout the world. Already his rule extended to Sidon and the
Sidonians, and he spread our city's power to Libya and to the Syrian coast.

Those were great days for Tyre! He brought cedar and gold to refurbish
the houses of Melkart, and filled in the sea to bring the god's ancient
temple within the city. What a marvel of a place that was! I watched him,

6.   Here Her Majesty seems to confirm the opinion of Katzenstein (1997: 126) that,
as the likely date of birth of Abdastratus is 948 BCE when his predecessor Balbazer,
son of Hiram (b. 961 BCE) was only 13, it seems likely that Abdastratus was the
younger son of Hiram, who was himself only 40 in 948.

7.   Here Her Majesty confirms speculation that the reference in Josephus to Jezebel
as coming 'from a line of kings' (*Ant.* 9.123) indicates that Ethbaal was connected by
blood to Hiram's line, a speculation supported by the close links between the
priesthood of Astarte and the royal house, and by the apparent ease with which Ethbaal
established his reign. He may even have been Abdastratus's son, though the likelihood
that the usurpers would have permitted the direct heir to live is plausibly questioned by
Katzenstein (1997: 130).

king and priest, sacrifice in the new temple. He brought me, too, his daughter, a trembling girl, to pay devotion to Astarte, the Mother whose service I adore.[8]

What I and Tyre owe my father, no one could calculate. Under his rule, we prospered as never before and Tyre grew in power and splendour. Our traders plied throughout the world. Kings courted him and even in Assyria they knew his name. He alone, from all the rulers of the cities of the coast, was invited to send guests to the celebrations of the new palace at Calah.[9] He sent ships of gifts in tribute to Shalmaneser III, and on the Gates of Balawat my father's portrait was embossed. He stands at the gate of our proud island city, while Shalmaneser receives the gifts of his friend and equal.[10]

It was in his reign, too, that we began to hear that another powerful man of war and vision, in favour with his gods, had come to power: Omri. The old king of Israel, Baasha, who had wiped out the family of his predecessor Jeroboam, died, and his son Elah came to the throne. He lasted two years, until a cheap assassin, Zimri, killed him while he was drunk, and destroyed his household in turn. Under the gods' wrath, Zimri lasted

8. Susan Ackerman (1999) argues that the queen mother, the *gebirah*, not only had a leading place in the political life of the Judaean court but was also in some way tied to a cult of the asherah which Ackerman argues was an accepted part of the royal cult in Judaea. Jezebel appears in this article as rather an exception, in that she is the only northern woman given the title *gebirah*. This may be explained by her status as the daughter of the Tyrian king, but also because dynastic succession was relatively rare in the Northern Kingdom anyway. During Jezebel's lifetime, the relationship between the Northern and Southern kingdoms was based on familial ties—Athaliah was Jezebel's daughter or step-daughter. In line with this idea, and Her Majesty's relationship to a king–priest of Astarte, Her Majesty is here expounding on her role as both priestess and in some sense representative of the goddess in the court of Samaria.

9. Katzenstein (1997: 133) cites an inscription of Ashurnasirpal II where only Tyre and Sidon are bidden to the official dedication. If Ethbaal was by this time king of both, he is the only invitee.

10. Here Her Majesty may be carried away to some extent. It is true that the tribute of Tyre is depicted on a bronze panel on the Gates of Balawat, and, unusually, it would seem that it is being delivered voluntarily, not under Assyrian duress (see Katzenstein 1997: 163-64; Pritchard 1978: 28-29, with a reproduction of the scene). Under the dating we are accepting for Ethbaal's reign, this campaign of 858 BCE occurred during his rule. However, the idea that this is a friendly gesture between equals goes too far. Ethbaal no doubt pre-empted an Assyrian attack by offering tribute, helped in this by the fact that, as an island, Tyre was more trouble than many other cities to take. At the same time, he secured the commercial future of Tyre.

only seven days until he too was killed by Omri, a just reward for a mere usurper—not even a royal nurse's son. Omri then had to fight for his throne, but he prevailed, and proved himself a worthy ruler. He set up a new capital for the kingdom and began to set the place to rights, with the help of his son, Ahab. He too was a man of vision, for an Israelite, and he knew my father's worth.

He knew too that to establish his kingdom he needed to outdo Jerusalem. There was no love lost, I can tell you, between these northerners and the descendants of David in their royal city in the south. It was Tyre, of course, who had provided the material and the craftsmen to build the temple and the palaces of the kings in the South. Ahab would have no less, and my father liked the cut of his jib. Under Omri's rule, the wealth of Israel had begun to build, and my father had an eye for trade wherever it was. Good relations with our southern neighbour could do us both no harm. Ahab was shrewd enough to understood our power and, seeking to embrace it on his own account, came to the house of Melkart and worshipped there. Returning to Samaria, he paid Tyrian craftsmen to build Melkart an altar in the royal temple and installed an asherah in honour of Astarte.[11] The destinies of our two people seemed to run together.

And so it was, that I, weeping with my maidens as I left my father's house, made that fateful trip to Samaria, and there met the man whose children I was to bear. I remember the day of my wedding where I wore robes of gold and many colours, flowing and scented with myrrh and aloes and cassia, followed by the daughters of kings and the sound of harps, as I came to the palace, gleaming in ivory against the wood. 'Forget your people and your father's house', they sang, as custom demanded.[12] I could not but smile, as I stood there in a house built by my father's workmen, surrounded by my father's ambassadors, hearing around me the language of my people, mixed with a few uncouth words from the hills. This *was* my father's house, in all but name, with familiar merchants who I had seen all my days living now in Samaria.

---

11. 1 Kgs 16.31-33: the odd phrase that Ahab '*went* and served Baal' (v. 31) has been taken by some commentators to indicate that he made the journey to Tyre. The identification of Baal here with Melkart is plausible, and biblical authors are not much concerned with the naming of foreign gods.

12. Ps. 45.10. This whole psalm at face value is part of the wedding celebrations of a king and a 'daughter of Tyre'. Ahab and Her Majesty are the obvious case to which this could refer, but any direct connection can only be speculative. Her Majesty's use of phrases taken from the psalm in this description reinforces the link.

But what a city—if you can call it that! Rough, uncouth and full of farmers, peasants from the hills, grubbers in the dirt. One hardly saw their like in Tyre. They feared the sea, but not as much as did the wild desert-dwellers with their crazy ways who would ride into town and look around them bewildered, clutching their meagre purses and flinching at every word. These hicks thought Samaria a frightening den of vice and theft. Samaria! Ahab and Omri did their best to make it a royal capital, but it was never Tyre, nor likely to be. The rabble looked on any woman with a sense of style as a harlot,[13] and instead of being awed or proud of what was built, their ignorant minds were filled with envy, stuck in the little limits of their squalid lives.

And worst of all, their prophets! Drunken peasants yelling out their malice in the name of their arid desert god, their brains baked with drought and sunstroke. We had prophets, Ahab and I, prophets to speak in the name of all the gods, dancing and singing and offering their blood as the gods' frenzy came on them in the temple. Baal, Melkart, Astarte, the gods who bring plenty, and bring justice, strong rule and good harvest. And Yhwh too, who was the god of Ahab's house and so of mine. I had no quarrel with Yhwh, nor he with me. When our two kingdoms wedded, our great and ancient Tyre with the new king's Samaria, what was more natural than that the wedding between Yhwh and his asherah should be affirmed, and that I, in my turn, should become the attendant to her rites in the temple?

These other prophets, though, were caught by desert demons. What kind of god dwells in the barren wilderness? Looking at his so-called servants, too, inspired little trust. That dismal dishevelled rabble of the poor was no advertisement for his power. And barren—this god of rocks and waste-land, how could he bring back the refreshing rains, and fill the ears of corn and the wombs of women? Look at their children, starved and wizened, dying like flies. A god of dust and ashes!

So I set to work, with Ahab's willing agreement, to bring the power of Astarte the mother of my city's god to this land. Most of the people seemed content with this. After all, their own god Yhwh had his asherah, and they thought like any farmers: whoever brought the rain would get their offerings and sacrifice. Some, however, clung to their desert super-stitions. None more so than Elijah, the gods' curse on him. A rabble-

---

13. Her Majesty would no doubt see her prejudices confirmed in prophetic passages such as Amos's denunciation of the 'cows of Bashan' (Amos 4.1-3) or the later Isaianic diatribe against the daughters of Zion (Isa. 3.16-26).

rouser, a blasphemer, a traitor and a skulker too. He had a fatal power over my husband, calling Ahab back to something deeply rooted in him from his ancestors, something with little time for cities and for kings. Remember that these people were from the hills. The pleasures and responsibilities of power were still new to them. Many expected to run an empire as if it were a village, where men could sit and gossip and discuss and where the elders were men among their equals. They had no understanding of the place of a king, who walks and speaks with gods and seeks their will and glory, not the crass opinions of men, who looks beyond his little land and deals for his god with the kings of distant places.

Elijah certainly understood nothing of this. He was a fool, an arrogant fool, and a coward too. From some desert hovel he appeared in a time of drought, and claimed that this disaster came and could be lifted at his bidding. Fool! Even that other skulking chancer Josephus tells the truth, though as usual in spite of his best endeavours. In order to show that Elijah had this power, he quotes one Menander, who clearly states that the drought was brought to an end by my own father Ethbaal praying to the gods![14] The gods no doubt withheld the rain so that it would not be polluted by falling on that crazed prophet's rags. I told my husband time and again that the goddess was displeased because her altars were neglected.

Yet Elijah preyed on Ahab's mind and when that traitor Obadiah brought the two together at last, Ahab did not kill the 'troubler of Israel', but actually agreed to send the royal prophets of Baal and Astarte to Carmel at Elijah's bidding. Though I swore vengeance, and wreaked it on Obadiah (search for his bones and his family if you will), it seemed a chance to trounce Elijah once for all. You can read the sorry story for yourself: how Elijah taunted the people for limping between two sticks, as if no one could see that two sticks give stability which one stick cannot guarantee. Then he arranged some spurious contest to see which of two bullocks could be burned, as if a god would consent to be tested! Baal did not answer, nor should a god come at the bidding of an unbeliever. What trick Elijah played, I do not know, but trick it was, with all a conjurer's cheap theatricality—buckets of water going up in flames! The rabble was convinced and, mad with power, Elijah slaughtered Baal's prophets by the stream. My poor deluded husband did not dare confront the frenzied mob and felt afraid, both of Yhwh's supposed power and Baal's silence. He

---

14. Josephus, *Ant.* 8.324. Josephus does rather seem to provide a hostage to fortune here!

told me all, however, because he knew Astarte would not brook the same insult.[15]

And did I make Elijah run! Off to the desert, where he belonged with the other jackals, though would I had caught him then! Brave with the rabble at his back, he knew my power and Astarte's and fled in fear. I gave him due warning, as I knew that killing him might turn the rabble on us. Killing the prophet of any god is a chancy business, but Yhwh's prophets left us no choice with their attacks on the gods and on the king. Reading these so-called histories of theirs, one might think I wiped them out, but even Elijah in all his vanity found he was not alone.[16] I was not such a fool as to stand against a god and his prophets. It was Elijah and his crew, who claimed Israel's royal god Yhwh as their own, who betrayed their god by setting him against Astarte and Melkart.

These prophets were a menace, but they could not even agree among themselves. My husband, weak though he was in the presence of the gods, was a mighty warrior. When that upstart Ben-hadad, king of Syria, sent his sneering message demanding that Ahab hand over his silver and his gold and his wives and children—including me, of course, the daughter of the Tyrian king!—the same Yhwh, who Elijah invoked against us, spoke through his prophet to give my husband victory and gain his cities back from the beaten Syrians.[17] Was this the act of a god who vowed vengeance on our house?

Ahab, I was proud to see, showed in this victory his growing understanding of the task of kings. He bound the vanquished Ben-hadad with a treaty which meant that his land and Israel and the lands of Tyre were all at peace and trade might flourish. Of course these ignorant prophets knew only one tune, and one of them again deceived the king, telling him in Yhwh's name that Ben-hadad was devoted to destruction and that he would forfeit the kingdom for releasing him.[18] They sought to use the king's respect for Yhwh to destroy the kingdom, and though Ahab knew this, something in him feared them too. Even that pip-squeak Naboth, as I said before, could play the card of tribal loyalty and unman the king.

In the end, through Elijah's accomplice Elisha, this treachery bore fruit.

15. There is a hint here that the fact that the 400 prophets of Asherah mentioned in 1 Kgs 18.19 seem not to be involved in the Carmel story might indicate that they took a different line. Of course, Her Majesty defends the goddess at every point.

16. 1 Kgs 20.18.

17. 1 Kgs 20.13.

18. 1 Kgs 20.35-43.

These prophets were a faithless crew, with no loyalty to their king or to the gods, and yet they accuse me of faithlessness! We were a family of powerful women, but we were faithful to the last. My poor great-niece, ill-fated Elissa,[19] whom you call Dido, shows our fortitude, even in that barbarian propaganda which justified the jealousy of upstart Rome for Carthage.[20] It took two gods all their powers to trick her into betraying the memory of her husband. Venus had to use her own son Cupid in the guise of Aeneas's boy to overwhelm her with an irresistible passion. Juno knew this when she upbraided Venus with her hollow triumph over the woman: 'One woman mastered by the arts of two immortals',[21] she called Elissa. Before the goddess interfered, Elissa vowed her love to her husband and uncle, the holy priest:

> He who first wedded me took with him, when he died,
> My right to love: let him keep it there, in the tomb, for ever.[22]

I gave my life, too, for the man I married and his kingdom. Samaria could have been a Carthage of the East, another great city, had I had my way. Yet, for all his folly, I was faithful to my husband. Never once, in all their

---

19.   Elissa is traditionally credited with founding Carthage. Katzenstein summarizes her story as it is found in the second-century CE *Epitome of Pompeius Trogus* by Justinus (see Katzenstein 1997: 187-89; also Herm 1973: 182-84). This is a late summary of an earlier history of the Phoenicians itself dependent on earlier Phoenician sources. Sister of the tyrant Pygmalion of Tyre, who was himself the grandson of Jezebel's brother Baal-azor, Elissa was married to her uncle Zakar-Baal, the priest of Astarte. Pygmalion, however, jealous of his uncle's wealth, had him murdered, and Elissa fled, accompanied by a few retainers. Eventually she landed in what is the present Carthage and became the queen of the city she founded. Legend also states that she was importuned by the king of Tunis, but rejected his advances and burned herself to death. It is a version of this legend which becomes the basis of her story in the *Aeneid*, book 4, to which Her Majesty alludes. Her Majesty's point is not so much the historical evidence. This, as far as can be determined, confirms the striking notion that these two remarkable women were close blood relatives, though their conjectural dates make it unlikely that they met. Rather, her point is to remind us that both women seem to show uncommon loyalty to their husbands, and yet stories arise around them which are erotic and which hint at faithlessness. Both become the archetypal 'foreign queen' in the literatures of their enemies. Both also are sacrificed so that another masculine dynasty can arise, almost as if the fertilizing blood and tears of a woman are necessary.

20.   Her Majesty's view of the role of Carthage is understandably rather different from Virgil's in the *Aeneid*.

21.   Virgil, *Aeneid*, Bk 4, l. 95 (Day Lewis 1966: 221).

22.   Virgil, *Aeneid*, Bk 4, ll. 28-29 (Day Lewis 1966: 219).

lives, did those Hebrew fanatics impugn my chastity; never is my name linked with any other man's. Their filthy tongues slavered over whoredom, often enough, because I was faithful, yes faithful, to my father's queen, Astarte.

When Ahab died, I took my place as *gebirah*, queen mother in my son Ahaziah's house. Now I see a presage of my own fate in Ahaziah's fatal fall through the lattice. It holds dark resonances for me. At my insistence, he sent messages to Baal-zebul of Ekron, a god I honour as his name echoes my own, to enquire whether he would recover. They came back, saying they had met a prophet who told them the king would die because he did not enquire of the God of Israel. When Ahaziah heard it was a man clad in haircloth with a leather girdle, we knew that once again Elijah had surfaced from wherever he was lurking. Three times we sent a party of soldiers to capture him, and three times they failed. The same trick with fire which won him the contest at Carmel burned and scared our men.[23]

Elijah got his just deserts however. Soon after, we heard that he had disappeared, leaving Elisha to continue his destructive blasphemy. Rumours began that he was taken up to heaven in a whirlwind with chariots and horses of fire in attendance. I do not know what to make of these tales. It was good riddance, however it occurred. If Elisha did not murder him—and who can trust these fanatics when they squabble?—then my belief is that long-suffering Baal finally dispatched his lightning and burned Elijah where he stood—that madman played with fire just once too often.

Still, his words came true, in that my Ahaziah died, without sons. Those were the words too, however, of Baal-zebul, who was incensed that messengers to him should be delayed and that the king should consider consulting Yhwh. The Hebrew scribblers omit to tell you that. Joram, his brother, took the throne, and showed himself a king. Those sheep-herders the Moabites rebelled, under the upstart Mesha, and Joram set out with that Southern fawner Jehoshaphat and the king of Edom to quell the rebellion. They ran out of food and water in that dry country and Jehoram was about to call a retreat, when, lo and behold, they encountered Elisha.

For a time, he had seemed to be content to roam with his rag-tag bands of prophets, and to track him down was too much trouble. He dismissed my son with unbelievable arrogance, or at least unbelievable from anyone but him, consenting only to speak to the Southern puppet. He did predict

23. 2 Kgs 1.

the rain, I give him that, but it was our soldiers who conquered Moab until king Mesha slew his own son on the wall, a desperate act which even that provincial tribal god Chemosh could hardly ignore. The wrath of Chemosh made it politic to retreat.[24]

After that Elisha grew bold, setting trouble between Syria and Israel.[25] At his behest, the King of Syria sent a threatening letter to my son, demanding that Naaman, his army commander, be cured of leprosy. My son rightly saw this as a challenge, but Elisha persuaded him to send Naaman to his house. A foolish act, it turned out, because thereafter the relations between Elisha and the Syrian army became suspiciously close. Naaman came to Elisha, and then returned to his master. Not long after, the Syrians began to attack Israel and Elisha was able to tell us of their plans. He then masterminded a capture of the whole invading Syrian army and persuaded the king to release them.

What strange unlikely collaboration between Naaman and Elisha is behind this? It only dawned on my son after the siege of Samaria when two women stopped him to squabble over the small matter of whose son they should eat in the midst of the appalling famine. Once again, Yhwh's prophets were conspiring against the kingdom, but not only against Israel. Elisha was playing with both kingdoms but Israel was bearing the brunt in this appalling siege. The prophets of the very god whose business it was to protect the kingdom and the king had turned against them. My son sent men to murder Elisha. When they failed, my son came himself to Elisha, railing against the faithlessness of Yhwh. Elisha turned the tables by prophesying the flight of the Syrians. The next day, the whole army was gone.

What did Elisha know? What had Naaman told him? The rumour that the Hebrew scribblers tell is that the Syrians fled because they heard the

24. Here Her Majesty gives a perhaps more plausible account of the event than the common interpretation of 2 Kgs 3.27, which suggests that Israel abandoned the siege in some excess of moral outrage, or even, following Josephus, out of pity for Mesha's situation (*Ant.* 9.42). She suggests it was a prudent decision to retreat once Mesha played the trump card of sacrificing his own eldest son. It was *Chemosh*'s wrath that might come upon Israel.

25. The history of these wars is confused to say the least. Here Her Majesty seems to take the biblical account fairly much at face value at least in chronological terms, but gives an interesting counter-reading of the motivation of the prophets. Her accusation of sustained anti-monarchism may reflect her own paranoia, but like many such tales achieves, at least to my mind, a surprising coherence. The relationship between Elisha, Naaman and the Syrian monarchy certainly raises questions.

noise of an army and though they were surrounded by Hittites and Egytians. Who spread that rumour, and how did it reach the ear of the Syrian commanders? In any case, there is a suspicious echo here of one of the old Hebrew stories of a hero they call Gideon, not wanting to acknowledge that he did his deeds in the power of Baal under the name Jerubbaal. He also made an army flee by night simply by surrounding them with his small band all blowing trumpets, smashing jars and waving torches.

What happened at Samaria, I do not know. What I do know is that Elisha brought down three kings thereafter. Was this an anarchic plot of those fanatics of Yhwh, who were never happier than when the whole world was a collection of warring and wandering tribes, refusing to settle into cities to find peace and prosperity? Ben-hadad was murdered by Hazael, at Elisha's suggestion, so rumour had it,[26] and Naaman said nothing. More deceitfully still, Hazael provoked a fight with both Joram and Ahaziah, king of Judah, my grandson. His mother was Athaliah, my daughter, another powerful woman of our blood who was to die by Hebrew treachery. Joram was wounded and carried to Jezreel, where Ahaziah came to visit him. I tended them both, unaware that Elisha had sent a minion to anoint Jehu king in my son's place, an act of breathtaking treachery and breach of law.

And so to my own end. The painted woman, 'wicked and abandoned'? Abandoned I was, alone in the palace at Jezreel, when news came that Jehu had slain my son, treacherously, on Naboth's field. A fitting place for yet another illegitimate usurper against his king's established rights to start his bloody reign![27] Not content with that act of murder, he slew Ahaziah too. When the news came to me, I saw my world was smashed. I will not satisfy you by dwelling on that moment, if your imagination does not already flinch before the thought of my anguish. I am the daughter, wife and mother of kings.

Then Jehu came in his wild-driven chariot and stopped before the palace. Here is a picture you all know. The old queen paints her eyes, puts

---

26. The biblical account in 2 Kgs 8.7-15 seems to show Elisha merely prophesying that Hazael will become king, but he is at least as implicated in Ben-hadad's death as the witches in Macbeth are in Duncan's, even on this account. That rumours of more active involvement would spread seems inevitable, and certainly the biblical account does lead us to wonder why the Syrian army shows no resistance to Hazael.

27. This is a characteristic counter to the biblical implication that Joram's death was a requital of Ahab's house for the death of Nathan (2 Kgs 9.25-26).

on her finery and greets the usurper from her balcony.[28] What do you imagine I was thinking? Those painted eyes have excited fevered minds from that day on, as if any woman worth her salt would meet her nemesis unadorned. Was this some simpering harlot seeking to seduce the new young lion, offering her body for her life? She would have been a fool, that woman, who knew the rage of Jehu and his kind. No, this was the goddess's handmaid, her chief of staff, arrayed as the goddess herself, taking her stand against the implacable hatred of the desert god.

'*Ha-Shalom?* Is it peace—can it be peace—between us?' were my first words to Jehu. To placate a new usurper, you do not name to his face, as I then did, his puny predecessor: Zimri, also a no one from the army, self-appointed king and dead within the week, a slave murdering his master. Was I afraid? Of what? My husband gone, my sons killed, all my house in peril—what more could I lose? One thing, and that one thing I kept and could still keep: honour, the honour of the goddess, and the honour of a Tyrian queen. Jehu knew I was alone, a woman, no longer young, and yet he stopped before me. For a long moment, his eyes met mine, and there I saw, behind disgust and battle-anger, a glint of recognition, a man who knew power and courage even in his enemies. Though my curse is on his bones and on his house forever, I saw that in him too. Here was the

28. 'The woman in the window' as a motif is discussed by Exum (1996: 72-75). She points to the prevalence of this image in the art of the ancient Near East and provides illustrations of two examples of ivories depicting this which may be from eighth-century Phoenicia. She discusses the motif in connection with the biblical story of Michal who observes David from a window (2 Sam. 6.16), but also recalls Sisera's mother who looks down from a window, waiting in vain for her son's return (Judg. 5.28) as well as mentioning this scene with Jezebel. The interpretation of this motif is uncertain—is the woman a prostitute, as some have argued, or is she the goddess? Whoever she is, Exum declares, she represents the woman confined, but also resisting her confinement, shut in but wanting to know what is happening beyond the walls of her sphere, the house. All three examples in the Bible concern a woman awaiting a man, though in rather different circumstances, a man who is returning from a significant event in the world beyond. We might make another series of connections with this scene, however, and compare Jezebel to David in 2 Sam. 18.24, waiting for news of Absalom, and the wounded Joram, Jezebel's son, waiting for the same Jehu. The verbal similarities between the encounter of Jehu and Joram (2 Kgs 9.17-24) and the encounter with Jezebel are striking, but redound to the credit of Jezebel. Her son seems genuinely so to misread Jehu as to sue for peace, and when realization strikes him, his response is flight. Jezebel's courage is only heightened by the narrative echoes.

makings of a man, deluded by the desert gods, but something like a man indeed.

Yet it took the unmanned to do me down, those whimpering eunuchs who dared to seize me and throw me from the balcony. My body struck the walls as I fell, leaving marks of blood, like the lamb's blood they daub on their lintels to ward off death's angel. Here's a pretty thing, to make me speak of my own death! Trampled by the horses' hooves and mauled by dogs, till only scraps were left. I hear the centuries' appalled yet eager gasp, and then the cheer as my ageing flesh is gnawed and snarled over.

Look at me, displayed for all to see in a canvas painted two thousand years on, by Giordano.[29] Fascinated, appalled, the lascivious lords of Naples took unclean pleasure in the rupture of ripe flesh. Jehu is there, stern, on a horse, an anachronistic knight, while others gaze or shrink to see the woman at last get her deserts from their implacable god. A god who uses dogs to do his dirty work. And there I lie, matronly, but handsome still, my dress rucked up to show one naked leg, the dogs about to start their work upon my breasts.

The painted woman. So men have stood as witches burned, as prostitutes and adulteresses were paraded in the streets and stoned, as errant daughters felt their fathers' wrath, as husbands, or Yhwh with his faithless Israel, beat and bruised and slashed the flesh that both compelled and repelled them. To you, perhaps, it is a fairy tale, the wicked witch baked in her own oven by Hansel and Gretel, or flattened by Dorothy's house in the land of Oz, only her feet showing, to the cheers of little, little people. Grotesquely, ridiculously, only my poor feet and hands were left, trophies for the house. Forgive me if I do not share the glee; if my woman's memories are all too real.

Do not mistake me. I know my hands had shed the blood of many, that my feet, too, if you like, had waded in the blood of those who sought to oppose me. Pain and dismemberment were no strangers to my rule. I gave and asked no quarter. But you, you who read this—what are you looking at when you look at me? Is it not the goddess, the mother, the wicked witch who thwarts, cajoles and ultimately betrays you, who you see die in me? Do I not carry every woman's burden where men allay their fears through wrecking women's bodies? Is it peace, you Zimris? I may ask again: Why dress me up again in plays, in books, in films, only to seek my

---

29. *The Death of Jezebel* by the Neapolitan painter Luca Giordano (1634–1705), reproduced in Gaines 1999 (pl. 6) and in colour in Bernard (1983: 109).

fall at eunuch's hands? What peace are you seeking? What peace do I disturb in you?

Jehu had both the ruthlessness and dignity not to watch, and did send out to have me buried as a queen. Yet there I was, or was not, spread across the earth like dung, he said, perhaps with a scribe's schoolboy humour sniggering at the pun. Degradation knows no worse than to be without a tomb, except to be without a name. My name has lasted these three thousand years. Dung, after all, spread upon the land, feeds it and will lead to growth, as the earth's flesh absorbs it. I at least am part and parcel of the land, receiving the benediction of Baal's seed the rain, as long as earth lasts. Baal, torn in combat, dies and rises again, as does Adonis or Osiris. I too am rent for the goddess's honour. And you, prophet; caught up in fire, consigned to the remoteness of the sky, no trace of you on earth? They wait for you I'm told. I can wait, too.

For who has won, Elijah? In the third millennium of the new age, numbered from the rising of another son of God done to death by treachery, is not the goddess, who can never die, returning to her own at last, showing weak and vicious men that all their violence and bluster can never change the fact that it is in the womb of women that the world is formed? Astarte, great mother, avenge at last your faithful daughter's death!

GHOSTWRITING ISAIAH

Francis Landy

I: this drift, this saying, I am, incarnation and cohabitation with so many bodies, this voice, never quite at home, that comes and speaks in the womb, come, be, belong, be filled with light and immensity, this immense labour, forming the words, the book, leaving it unsettled, to work its strange work, in you, who are also me, in whom I cohabit, sometimes, this book, this strange book, to which I belong, which is me, so unfinished, so unsettled: we, once, before the word, the voice, we once…were.

I, Isaiah ben Amoz, he wrote me, in the days of Uzziah, Jotham, Ahaz and Hezekiah, kings of Judah, those phantom kings, whose lives slide off the shuttle, so swift, so immemorable, they were. My father, Amoz—but was he really my father? my father, they say, was God, who bespoke me, in the silence, whose voice and word I carry—my father, Amoz, strength, shadow, silence. The father who passed into the shadows, quickly, crypted. And my mother, even more shadowy, not even a face or a name, but she is everywhere, Mother Zion, Mother Jerusalem, the empty, bereaved mother, the mother I have bereaved, I cannot recall. The mother of flesh, the anxious, waiting, laughing mother. My mother. The mother with whom I learned to speak, in whom I hear myself echoed, the first word, words, all this I have forgotten. My brothers and sisters too, impressions barely, long tangled lives, some. I loved perhaps: time, sunlight, the solitary courtyard. Days speak, nights speak, and people whisper their words.

My childhood, before the saying came to me, before I was, was it ever mine? A childhood beyond the tumultuous ages, loved by the good world, before anything happened. Before war. You perhaps can imagine, you have your own thresholds. It hasn't changed, in some ways. The vineyards stacked in terraces round the mountains, the olive groves deep in the valley bottoms, the gardens, the wheat fields, figs, pomegranates, women coming, inexorable as shadows, to pick the fruit in the early dawn. Nebi Samwil looked over us too, a sacred place, to the prophet Samuel. We too ate grapeleaves, stuffed with chickpeas, dill, barley, meat. Cattle trampled the meadows; sheep filled the evening air with their clamour. Ours was a prosperous house, blessed by the Lord. People looked at us with pride, felt at ease with us. Our labourers shared in our well-being, they were our people. We planned, knew, spoke not hastily, followed the plough across the heavy fields.

It is not sweet nostalgia that makes me talk, that squeezes my heart with the desire to return. It was truly untroubled; I could not go there without bringing my trouble with me, like the town of Laish so long ago. I want to keep it back there, unvisited, safe. I want to taste my mother's milk, in the deep recesses of my mind, unpoisoned. Everything admixed with bitterness, with longing.

There was death in that world too. Sometimes I hear nothing but weeping, when I think of those times; the lamenters; the drinking feasts, when people would stagger bewildered; fevers. The shadows on people's faces never disappeared. The dead had their dwelling close to us. Our dead, however: how can I remember so little? I cannot tell you the anniversaries, the dates, of my father's and mother's deaths. I cannot tell you if they died; I cannot remember their deaths. The death of children, so remote, so chilling, at an impossible distance. I want to remember them, to claim them, to light lamps and pour offerings, to insert myself again into a human world.

You have no idea what it was like. You have so many strange ideas about us. I cannot tell you what it is like to be where everything fits into place. Imagine. Listen. Perhaps my poetry is a way of listening to the sounds, things minding their business on all sides. The chirping of the cricket like that of a ghost. The dry grass in my throat.

Reading, writing…the father disciplines his son, the teachings are inculcated in the children. You think of the voice of admonition painfully reproduced. I learned to read and write, words and voices becoming visible under my hand. Even then I sensed the power and danger of writing, a trap for voices, an impression of the world like the impression of the seal in wax. It was part of learning what it was to be human, to assume responsibility for our value and future. Reading and writing placed us at the centre of things, as administrators and thinkers; the accomplished person was one who knew how to act on the basis of what was thought. Anybody who wished to be anybody could turn a phrase, amid the other pleasures and marks of civilization. But it was more than that: we were passionate about knowledge, about truth.

Writing was everywhere; bits of papyrus, inscriptions on walls, jars, metal, scrolls of parchment or leather, clay and wooden tablets. Not just the exiguous tale that has come down to you. The project of writing the history of our people had not yet begun. There were so many narratives, versions of narratives. The air was thick with stories. We collected them, just as we did proverbs, psalms and everything else. We heard singers at the markets and crossroads, we listened to itinerant prophets and teachers, whose words were recorded, by themselves, by disciples or paid copyists, so that their words would not vanish, their reputation would spread.

Behind all the stories was the figure of Moses, who led the people through the wilderness, the land of exhaustion and vision. I was born there, I was found, the voice of Moses, the voice of the wilderness, heard in silence and desolation. I am born again and again, Lilith they call me, the voice of God. Nothing and nowhere is home. I am the man of God, the servant of that which is other and beyond human authority. I see nothing, only the years immerse themselves in my still eyes, leaving not a trace. I raise my staff and shatter the words against the rock.

We came from Egypt, slaves to Pharaoh, builders of cities. You think that is myth, retrojection of the future, my future, the festival of Passover indeed a passage to a new, redeemed community, when I came back to Zion, like a dreamer. Indeed, but for us the past was haunted. We did not belong here. It was not our land, our dead. And then we would wake up and look at our fields and vineyards in the sun, and tell ourselves it was a good world. Rubbing our eyes.

It was a world inhabited by many peoples. You think we were insular, off the trade routes, of not much interest to anyone. You will read of our xenophobia, the evils of foreign women, not to speak of deities. But it wasn't like that. An educated person would learn, travel. We lived between civilizations. There were resident Egyptians, Phoenicians, Aramaeans in our cities; we had merchants and diplomats. One could learn Egyptian, Assyrian, Ionian; one could read not only our literature, but those of our neighbours.

As a young man, I too travelled. What else should one do in a small country? We had connections with Tyre—business friends of my father—traders in wheat, wine and oil, spices and timber. They brought with them a knowledge of the world, the expanse of the ocean and the myriad peoples, that nourished my imagination; our lives had an affinity and a mutual ease, a shared concern, more profound than business considerations and ethnic affiliations. For us, Tyre was the gateway to a breadth of outlook, a common culture, a variety of experience and a richness of encounter by which one became a man of wisdom. Our kingdoms had been allied, through marriage, joint expeditions, and building projects, for several generations, before the invasions disrupted all political stability. Our friends had not only trading interests here; they were devotees of Yhwh of Jerusalem, and came to bring offerings, to learn, to gaze upon his light. From them I had my first intimation of a world transformed by the divine presence, that my habitual designation, 'the Holy One of Israel', in fact embraced all peoples. But that was for the future.

I went down to Jaffa and embarked on a vessel for Tarshish. The fabulous tale that you know, the prophet who ran away from Yhwh and from himself, can give you some idea of the magic of the word, the terrors and wonders of the sea. Huge fish, you call them tuna and shark, swam in schools; beyond the western gates whales were sometimes stranded and butchered. Dolphins and porpoises leapt, and swordfish glided. On land there were megaliths, elephants, snowy mountains, and the wealth and ingenuity of mines. I saw everything with joy: the sun on water, the white harbours, the brilliant cities, people, women. Sex assailed my nostrils and my guts. More than sex, more than sight, was language. Everywhere people talked—and sang. I was stationed for three years, as an agent of the firm, on one of the Ionian islands—Chios, Lesbos, I forget. I learned to speak, of course; I knew the singers, I learned the songs: love, and war, the harmonies of lyre and voice. All night people drank and listened to the poets, the long stories of sea and land, the epic of the Trojan War, and I thought back to my own land, my own rhythms in my own tongue. How to speak of the sea in Judaean? How to let sun, and brilliance of light on water, shine in my voice also? The shining, appearing, of beings. The beautiful bodies of boys and girls, can I forget the desire that overwhelmed me? To make flesh appear in stone, in all its transience and perfection, and be immortal. Even now I am assailed with longing, for that other world. That possibility. In the morning lizards would scurry between the white houses. I blessed God, or was it the gods, was there a difference between God and the gods, Ionians, Tyrians, Judaeans, my friends in all worlds? I was free of my burdens, the trade, the work, the sweetness in my blood. In the morning those who had listened and danced slept late, complained, as if the music had left them behind, like wreckage on the shore.

I would go back to Judah. It was my home, the familiar, yet always seen with different, alien eyes. I beheld the slave and horse markets of Egypt, the perfumeries, the fishermen in the Nile, with their fragile craft. In Egypt anything could be bought, and the whole world met. You think we were religious, all of us, bringing sacrifices, singing psalms, sure of our national destiny, Egyptians as well as Judaeans and Babylonians. You don't know much else about us, about what we thought and imagined. Indeed, God was at the centre of our lives. Yet my fundamental preoccupation was not God. Perhaps that is true of all of us, at least insofar as we meet and speak of what matters to us. I wanted to know what it meant to be human, how to lead our lives, with truth, and probity, and wisdom.

Words came to me, fragments of phrases, a music. I was never without that voice. Yet it was born in me at a specific time and place. That of course is an exaggeration. I was always aware of invisible beings, I could always be past or future, or elsewhere. Our world was haunted, not only by the dead, but by signs and portents. The lion roars, my friend Amos said, and who does not tremble? I've always felt an affinity for lions, as if we prophets were lions, by other means. Once I looked into a lion's eyes. We met only a few feet apart, each as surprised as the other. It turned away, and instantly could not be seen. I have rarely felt such intensity of encounter. The eyes, a shock of light and then a haze, an aureole, imparted to me a gravity, a solemnity, amidst the power and heat, the violent life of the world. Dryness, crackling, silence. Our eyes became one for a moment. And then it was gone.

Lion of God. The lions cry, outside. And inside, in the palace, the hearth, the holy of holies, Ariel. I trembled all over, from the power and awe of it. The lion speaks within me.

We belonged to a spiritual elite, so we felt. Priests were among our friends, wise men, learned in the traditions. The king was distantly related, though we were not intimate. We kept to our own ways, our own house: trade, friends, travel, field. It is odd to recall what it felt like to be Judaean, to belong to Jerusalem. To be at the centre of the earth, to watch the sun rise over the Moabite mountains, to hear the nations crashing at our feet. We had our pride in being chosen of God. Our city was the most perfect, the most beautiful on earth. Our king was anointed by God, and his line would last for ever. We even felt superior to those people who lived in Samaria, kith and kin, who shared our expectations, our traditions, our deity. Ours was the true line, while they were renegades, secessionists. Such absurdity. I love Jerusalem, our fields, our past. But I am not born there, I do not die there. I die in you, and in you. You know what it is to love a place, to think it mother, blessed, holy. You sing your songs, stand up for your anthems. I am heard in all your voices. I have heard the slave songs, the shanties, the lamentations for Jerusalem and Babylon. Warsaw. Prague. *El mole rahamim*. Only the voice rises from the ashes, my voice.

We worship the one God, Yhwh, the invisible, the infinitely secret, the washer of the world, as one of his poets—Jeremiah, Celan—said. The name is like a breath, a wind, taking us away into the silence. I can almost smell him, in the stench of the sacrifices and the slaughter-houses. His name is infinite, illusion, Maya. He smells of roses, the pale flesh whitening in the spring. I see him in the hedge roses. You have your own conceptions. You know a lot about us: the horses of the sun, Yhwh and his Asherah, the worship of the state and the king, those things that made us no different from any other nation, our God from any other god. I felt the precariousness of our existence, our images, that Yhwh nullified all gods, all cherished realities. I knew he could be found in the desert, in the silence, in the shade of a dark rock.

I apprenticed myself—I was quite old, in my mid-twenties. My teacher had travelled too, in search of knowledge. He knew of other peoples who distinguished falsehood and truth, imposed absolute moral requirements, for whom all old gods and images were vanity and illusion. He had been an ascetic, a Levite, who knew what it was to depend on others. Now he lived in Jerusalem, in an empty house; his wife had died, and he had no children. The solitude settled around him, but he was not lonely, for he lived cautiously, guarding his resources, and in the presence of Yhwh. Besides, he was visited constantly by disciples, colleagues, people in need of advice or a blessing. His solitude was a reserve, somewhere set aside within himself, a quietness in which one felt oneself at home, in repose. I thought of him later, as an intimation of what we might have been, what I might have been, if things had been different. Everything about him was very clean: his house, his hair, his clothes, his body. One bathed before visiting, as a sign of respect. It was a place, a person, in which Yhwh had his dwelling. I too bathe each day, my clothes are laundered, for I too stand in his presence. I am very fond of the fullers' field, as you might know. They are like God, the washerwomen; I befriended them and would watch them, their chapped hands, their songs, their pride in their work. The best lye in the world came from near Jericho. We prophets were very conscious of the dignity of our profession; we were more than priests. One would not touch a sacred scroll without washing; we held the living word.

So to visit my teacher was to visit God, and we felt awe, emanating from his eyes and hands. But he was a very unassuming person, round-faced, younger than his years, resilient, with brown still interspersed in his grey hair. There was an automatic friendship between us; I felt myself his successor, his prophet, his emissary. All that is of course illusion. There are no prophets, there is no succession, no voice to speak of, only this silence. His name, before he entered the silence, Uriahu. But he has no name.

We travelled, walked through the land, went on pilgrimages, the usual things, Gilgal, Peniel, Beersheba—you know them. The journey more than the place, clamorous and full of discord. We went to Horeb, and the cave of the echoes. There, if you listened closely, you could hear the reverbera- tion of revelation, the hidden speech that summoned the world into existence. It was very still. Outside, the sage bushes hummed with it. But I heard nothing. Nothing asked me what I was doing there. We left our offering, flour, dried fruit, before the small shrine. The angels pecked at them. In the white heat their black silhouettes rose again and again, as devouring a corpse. We had no meat. Uriahu did not eat meat. It was not good for prophets to eat meat; it made the body coarse and violent. A prophet had to be transparent to God. He was a sign of the age in which there would be no violence, there would be peace between animals and human beings. That's why they lived long. I myself have not followed that rule. I eat what befalls me. I speak of the age in which I live.

Every Sabbath the prophets of Jerusalem, and neighbouring cities, would meet in Uriahu's house, or the house of another prophet. They would eat and drink; we apprentices would serve them, and watch from the shadows. They would read, discuss, a text, Torah. Here was God's speech, here is where we founded ourselves. The text was our defence against confusion and chaos. Incest, for instance, was the very metaphor for chaos. You know those long and hideous chapters, in your Bible, they are rooted in ours. 'Your father's and mother's nakedness you shall not uncover', for they are the root of all. They shall be planted in the earth, to grow and be forgotten. They are the face of God. I know what it is to see the face.

Uriahu taught me to read. To read for the most hidden implications, for the music of the letters, for the spirit of the one, the one, who wrote. To watch the letters disappear invisible into the depths from which they came. Letters are pathways for the one who knows. We could count them, trans- pose them, perceive their secret symmetries. They are things, elements, performances, in ceaseless combination. We would read black for white, space for silence, the gaps between the letters. Uriahu taught me to concentrate on one text, a few lines, for many months. It became living matter, shape, sound. And was divested of those properties, until it was pure letter, the slightest movement and trace of breath.

After the reading, the different opinions, the shadows in the text, we sang—songs of celebration, you know them as Psalms. There were many more than one hundred and fifty, of course. Songs for the Sabbath. On the Sabbath there could be no grief. I remember their voices. They were expert at voices, women and men, young and old. The strongest prophets could sing in many voices. I myself learned the purest voices, there in the desert: the voices of demons, the screech owl, Lilith, the jackal, the hyrax, the grasshopper. There were voices without words, without bodies. Migrating birds would leave their voices, swallows, storks, those huge flocks passing without ceasing.

One can sing without words, one can sing in silence. As the voices departed, we continued listening. From a great distance one would speak of the word that had come to him, or to her, of the dreams and encounters that had passed through us. Sometimes, out of the depths, Yhwh would speak, the vocables tumbling out, fractured, and sometimes resonant with power and beauty. That was rare. For years one of us might be silent; one had to maintain one's vigilance, responsibility, knowing that it would come when least expected, under the eyelashes. Sometimes the word would waylay a person, like a robber or a lion in ambush. We thought at times that we were all one voice with many branches. I too know the burden of silence, exhaustion.

They would speak also of what was happening in the world, passionately, in their normal voices. I got to know of the world of politics on those Sabbaths. And suddenly all was over. In the midst of argument one might start, whirl, dance. Sometimes all the participants would entrust themselves to the movement, the light pouring from hands and faces, barely visible in the beauty and immensity of the dance. We entrusted ourselves to the ages; the light pours ceaselessly, momentously. Justice, anger, pain, the demands and responsibilities of our profession, entered, provoked, and were erased in the dance. For the dance was death.

Outside spun the ordinary light, gracious in its innocence: light on stone, rain on roofs, down gutters, into the world of the dead. It was so familiar to walk home, to my parents' house, to the dwelling of the dead, the faces and memories of childhood, to feel the leaves by the roadside, to watch the grain and the grapes ripening, everything in its time, and to know that time vanishing. The huge sun disappeared in speech. I sang, 'our vineyards in blossom', in the consciousness of the other voice. In those days I could sing.

I learned to dream, and to sleep. Prophets were experts at sleep. For in sleep the mind opens, and in an instant one travels. No ship goes as far as the mind. The dream comes in the midst of words—who said that?—we spoke in the knowledge of the dream beyond speech. I slept a great deal; the master of proverbs, the industrious sage, would disapprove. I slept, I fasted, I gazed at the sunlight, the dust, the desert hills, I listened. Everything was a release of being, the jubilee of the soul. The prophet learns passivity, to vibrate to the merest touch. I know those paths. If I speak of the dust, it is because I know the dust living, suspended, in its own gravity, its own clear apprehension.

My apprenticeship to Uriahu continued for about three years. My family understood that this was my vocation, that I had the capacity to be one of the greatest prophets, but it troubled them. There were no prophets in our family. To be a prophet risked a social ambivalence; prophets did not quite belong in our world, you never knew where you were with them. I realized a discomfort with my family and friends I had never felt before. Even a sip of wine seemed unfamiliar. So I quit. I went back to the normal world. I married, had children. I can hardly remember that marvellous, humdrum interlude. You know how much I love children. To get up in the morning, to walk with them in the welcoming fields, to show them things for the first time, to hear language for the first time. Every father must know this. I loved pregnancy; our births were easy. My wife knew I must go away. She fought for me, and I fought together with her. I wanted her peace, her serenity, to make my nest by her side. Like the swallow and the turtledove, I thought. For once in my life I was not called. She too had the mantic gift, the capacity to hear the divine word, she had been part of the circle of Uriahu. We talked in the evenings, when the great house was empty, sleeping. There was of course a loveliness, a rootedness, in being part of a family. Some of my successors never had that. We read together, in the evenings, domestic bliss you might say, except that awe, the message from the other side, was always in waiting. Sooner or later I would disappear into darkness. She could have been I; perhaps our words are tangled together. Maybe in my prophecy you intimate her pale reflex. I bury myself in her flesh; she would embrace me, quickening to me. Such things are hardly to be remembered. You know how hard it is to describe someone. Our very own Song of Songs attests to that. Her image never leaves me, torments me, in the shadows, my dry voice longing for her hair, our children.

I walk between the stooked rows, and the dust clings to my throat. The gladness fades from trees and mountains, the tight clusters of the vine like children. I know it is afternoon. The lizard stares at me as if I were invisible. Suddenly, in the immense stillness, I see the lion, its eyes wide with recognition. I am very tiny. It seats itself, and regards me placidly. I might be, I am, a bird. With all my strength, dragging my flesh, I traverse the tufts of grass and stone to pat its mane. It vanishes in light.

And the sky opened, and the earth opened, and I heard the voice of my Lord. I am empty, I cannot be human, I can never again know child, or wife, or pleasure, without that emptiness, the hollowness where everything echoes for ever. It sucked in the silence, the bitterness, sky and earth, the beautiful bodies of men and women. In the wind, the whirlwind, the isles of the sea clattered like stones. This is the day of the Lord, I know. This is the end. And where can I hide myself, what particle of dust has room enough, when he rises to terrify the earth?

I heard the voice of my Lord saying, and gathered round the debris of my life, my ancestors, my clothes, to the saying. The grasshopper listened, erect on its stem, its dull body thrumming to the sorrow. And I heard. Nothing. No one. No one speaks in the silence. I am the grave of a voice. The nullity of desire.

I called, in my utter loneliness, my God, I am, mouth opening and closing soundlessly. My hair shrieks on end, fingers of lightning pluck it like strings. My body is fire and light, and I walk in the blazing grass. Animals come to me and I bless them. My feet are straight and molten and do not touch the ground. I am torch and crevasse, the rivers of ice gliding past like air.

A great lassitude befell me. I lay on the ground and waited for the world to return to its place, for the fires to damp down. When they came to get me, I could not recognize their burnished faces. They are the pall-bearers, I thought. They took me to the house on the swaying, heavy cart; it was so sweet to be drowsy. My wife knew what had happened; I roused myself and looked at the house, the glowing inner courtyard rank with memory. I lay on my bed and let darkness take me. My voice startled me, with my need for water, my hunger. Never had the world seemed so intense; the shimmering water, the rivulets of the body. Nothing seemed so precious, so passionate to be reclaimed. I could see the inner organs shining, the slow passage of the faeces, the burning exit of urine. Voices would rasp and cheep; this is what we sound like to the dead, I thought. The voices of the children filled me with desire and anxiety. In my prostration, I learned what it was to be worm, to be soil, to be moulded helplessly by the hand of God. My wife, Talia, cleaned me, washed me, fed me with a spoon, slowly, drip by drip, morsel by morsel. She pressed cold compresses, and my fever abated, little by little. My forehead was like an organ, more intimate than penis or vagina, a pathway for the flow of the pulse, the stream of pain and solace. The forehead, for you, is a metaphor for hardness, for stubbornness of will; you speak of being headstrong. But for me it was infinitely flexible, transparent, a sieve through which everything was clarified: thoughts, feelings, imagination, love. For the first time it was as if I could feel without body, communicate through blood alone. Communicate without communicating, without the clumsiness, the interposition of flesh. Perhaps this is what it is to be an angel, to be God. The foetus I was then. Talia and I, one flesh hardly, skin and indwelling. I would watch the clarified butter drain through the mesh. So soft the skin, and the silence spread between us, like the canvas of the sky. The light was the lamp, the soul and the blood. One day a man will graze a cow and two sheep. Our bodies so close, so interpenetrating, lay in the darkness; nothing came between us so feverishly as the desire for life. My reclusive body opened, claimed beginning; we held ourselves intact, our frail silhouettes against the wall.

Uriahu came, as I watched the children, one afternoon, playing in the sand. The fever relented day by day, every so often returning, like an obsession or a recurrrent dream. Sun was good for me, light was good for me; I was able to go for short walks. I saw Uriahu as I came back from one of these, in my fearful weariness, as I watched the children building and rebuilding houses, walls, a whole world sketched and crumbling. He walked through the dust and heat as if on a mission. But it was Talia who had sent for him, when I was prostrate with sickness, in her desperation. They talked a great deal, then and later, walking on the paths of our land, and in the stillness of the house. He liked it here, and we were glad of his presence. I roused myself from my torpor, called for water, embraced and kissed him. He was my master: how could I have been so bold? Gently we sat down together and we talked. I told him of what I had seen and heard—and that I heard nothing, felt nothing, the terror of being unable to speak, and he opened his mouth and cried, his mouth always clean, his teeth white as stone; I loved him then, loved his beard, his face, his round fierce eyes, I loved him more than I loved earth and sky, everything fell away, from the hair of my head to the sole of my feet, how could it come to this? how could it thus be? And we walked, in the darkness, through the councils of the gods, I knew those councils, those susurrations, through the dark stones between which the waters ran, to the secret dwelling, and there we waited, so that the imageless should become manifest, should speak. There the master of prophets came to us, our teacher, a knowledge among the dreams of knowledge, the one who knew the ways of God. He showed us the way into the house, the inner chamber.

There Yhwh spoke in my heart. The words unfold like leaves, they burrow deep in the flesh. He spoke of betrayal and sorrow, how it grieved him in his heart. He spoke with many voices, like the sea, and I recognized and untangled the voices. I am the voice, the undoing. Once I was a rock, struck by the hand of the prophet.

He spoke of love, the song of my beloved in the darkened city. The Asherah parting in the early light. I heard her forsaken voice in the streets of Tyre. I knew her in the sea; she walked in the deep melodies of whale and the flutes of dolphin. Her glittering dress was the ocean; the sun spread her skirts on the waves. He offered her half his kingdom. He told stories of the beginning, the venture into creation and speech. Before nothing was, no grass, no herb of the field, no answering voice, no thought. He spoke of light, and the music of the stars. Rahab woke again in his voice, once again there were sea battles, the waves crashing over him. I listened to myself, born again and again. Once again Abram set forth for a strange land, in high spirits, hardly noticing the earth on which he trod. Once again Jacob strove with God. In your Bible, it is all so clear, so linear. The city with its streets, line by line, echo by echo. But we do not have this. We have the birth from the inner chamber, the torment, the procreation. Moses led us there, between the rocks, to the secret place, where God touches himself, names himself. The garment of events torn to shreds: here is the flesh in its loveliness. Press it, press the petals.

He spoke of his love for his child, and the long accumulation of resentment. You know it well, with it I begin my book: 'Sons I have reared and exalted, and they have rebelled against me.' But what sort of love is it that cannot delight in the beloved? The pride of a father in his child, that I felt that afternoon as I watched and played with my children, allowing them to grow into their own bodies and their own lives: had he ever felt that? When the stars of morning sang all together, perhaps then: but was there not too much unanimity in their song? And who composed it? Perhaps a star may have inserted a note of parody, of wilfulness…?

And we, were we not created by him with that capacity to take pleasure? and cannot he do so? When the Asherah turned away from him in the early light, was it because he could not love? And he, consumed with rancour, summons and destroys the memory of her body, her symbols, her pillars, because he could never touch her, with the imagination that allows the flesh to become cloud and petal? The self-assurance of all things, in themselves, in their pride and beauty. The pride of David in his son, the glory of his flesh, did God know what that meant? Did he take pride in the long hair of Samson, the head and shoulders of Saul, the beautiful eyes of David?

All events were inscribed there, all words spoken, and I stood waiting, with horrible foreboding, while the voice shifted, addressed me directly, spoke of the prophets, the prophetic task and patience, the ceaseless call, as if listening to a speech it could scarcely understand, waiting for the clarification, and for the torpid movement of the heart. My ears amplified each chord, like blows, while my eyes grew accustomed to the darkness. I could see sound as light, as energy, and my whole body was radiant with it. I knew the prophets, Samuel the Seer, Elijah the Undying; I whirled in a dance with them. The master of prophets stayed still at the centre, as if he were a glass through which the light burned. The shadows, the silences, fall here and there; only they make it possible to salvage the moment, to say I, I am, to write the book.

I saw the Face, shining between the cherubim, a face fleetingly visible as the darkness reformed, my eyes closed in terror. It was no face, a visible thought almost, a passion. I shall die for this. I shall die never. For my eyes have seen. Yes. Yes. I passed through the councils of the gods, with Uriahu by my side; the susurration departed from me. Water trickled under my feet. And I beheld the living light.

Thus began my work as a prophet, housing the voice, that which speaks, is sealed. Body after body is discarded by the voice, like the transparent casings of insects, but while I live I must harbour it, keep it safe, and pass it on. Uriahu did so. And he felt free of his burden, at least for the months that he stayed with us. A Uriahu without authority. Who shared our lives without judgment, without the claim of the other side. To all appearances, little had changed, at least at first. I recovered my health, felt indeed a clarity of well-being, a freshness of existence, such as children might feel before the world becomes familiar. I have often seen this with those who have passed through profound sickness, who have touched death and returned. Is it true also of the dead? Outwardly, prophets lead their lives.

But I had already departed, to come back, again and again, to remind myself what it was before the wreckage, to say Talia, trying out the word with my tongue, before I departed forever. To be the wife of a prophet is not felicitous. My successor Ezekiel's wife died of the silence. It is like being married to a dream.

Once again Uriahu and I walked through the land, learning the paths that led from place to place, from story to story. I was no longer his disciple; I was the young prophet and friend of Uriahu; if you like, I was the future of the profession. I would contribute to the style of prophecy in the next generation; people, and especially prophets, looked at me with curiosity. Between Uriahu and myself the love, the companionship, had become a point of divergence; he could now slowly retire into ordinariness, while my advent, my commissioning—the one that you all know and celebrate daily—awaited me. He taught me everything that matters in our vocation. To listen. Not only to God but to human beings, to the quietest, subtlest, least-heard voices, to those who turn to us, in supplication, desperation, for advice and blessing. To the rich, the human heart trapped in its splendour, its possessions. To listen to the state of the land and its affairs. We travelled the length and breadth, from Dan to Beersheba, listening to the grievances, follies and dreams of our con-temporaries. Those things I had heard about politics, on those Sabbath afternoons in Uriah's house, now began to have substance, abundant illustration. We could sit in a corner, observing unseen; we could speak so that everyone would listen. Trust a prophet to know more than a king, for the king is blinded by desire. That is the second thing Uriahu taught me: to speak. To speak out of conviction, in the knowledge of the many voices that fill the world. To speak in the name of the Lord.

We know what it is to be poor, for on our travels we were utterly in-digent. There were many of us: Levites, prophets, strangers, the landless—you know the list, like a refrain—who depended on charity, who lived outside the well-marked boundaries of the fields, as it were, outside the social hierarchy. To leave behind the familiar landmarks by which one knew oneself, to cease to be a dispenser of goods, of goodness, to be the privileged landholder of your texts, on whom rests the responsibility, the plaudits, of divine benevolence, always reserving enough and more for oneself and one's own. I was Isaiah, son of Amoz, all my connections intact, and I was a mere stranger. You can imagine that to be a prophet, like being a Levite, an alien, a widow and orphan, a Nazirite, incurred disparagement. We were fed at the gate, as the saying goes, but not inside it. Popularly, prophets were madmen, frauds, scratching a living from the credulous. It is nothing new that I am saying. I was recipient, open mouth, like the raven in the Psalm. And to know hunger, physical necessity, that is to know also the hunger for language, the speech that poured into us, to be container, empty of self, of me, Isaiah son of Amoz.

Worst of all was the smell of our unwashed clothes, worn and colourless, the itch in the scalp and hair, the sweat drying on us day by day. We washed when we could, at springs and troughs, people would give us to bathe hands and feet, they would know, if we were prophets, we might wish to immerse ourselves. Remember Uriahu's house. But here it was impossible to escape the filth, the flies, the excrement in the fields. We knew the impurity of our people in our nostrils, and in our own bodies. Often we stayed in hovels crowded with children, with babies. Unswept, the dirty food mingling with the odours of the bucket. Sickness was worst: the inescapable vomit.

We travelled, nonetheless, and the beauties of landscape, of flowers, the violent contrasts of our land opened up to us. Mountain and plain, crocus, iris and lily, wood and desert, find their voices in me. We met groups of prophets, of poets, manifold dream worlds. We exhausted the visions in the sullen heat. And Uriahu taught me to write, forced the pen into my hand at the end of a long abrasive day. Pen and ink was the one necessity we could not ignore. We carried our scrip in our bundles, and our words in our head.

You think it is easy to write, you imagine that we prophets composed by inspiration. Or were drudges of convention. You have no idea how many revisions it requires to produce a worthwhile poem. How much pain. The dread of sterility, the headaches. For months I would shape, change, find the right word, declare it wrong, shift the images, escape, escape. Uriahu was always at my side, implacable in judgment. Gradually I learned my craft, to harness my strange voice. I became bold. But I knew also the seduction of poetry, writing without terror, without faithfulness. Always one goes back to the Face that is also my face, to the pure thought glistening. I learn to listen ever more closely to the words, to endure them, to pare them into human speech. I am fire, the letters are fire. If it were not for the predecessors, what you call tradition, taking me by the hand to the brink, I would have succumbed. Of loneliness, vacancy. The lion would have devoured me, as in those stories of the prophets. If it were not for love.

They took me, silently, to where we become nameless, silent. Even the name of God becomes breath and ash. And from the ash I drew my pen, and dipped it again and again, into the fire, scratching, erasing, scratching, that it should be indelible, that at last we should understand. The fire etched into my flesh, branding the name, the nameless.

Nevertheless, we were something new. In Samaria I met a prophet, Amos. I have already mentioned that he was my friend. Grey, with a slight hesitation of manner. In another age, he might wear a threadbare sweater. He was exiled, or had exiled himself, from Judah, goodness knows why. You know his famous self-effacement. But then no one is anything. Amos had an irremediable hopelessness, an impotent desire, against which I have always struggled. He taught it to me; it still seeps into my bones. For us, and I include Hosea and Micah, of those names you know, the continuity of history, our history, was at an end. Prophets need no longer warn particular kings or dynasties of their demise, in the assurance that life continues. And does it? Israel would indeed be annihilated, but so would Ethiopia and Caphtor. Remember how untroubled that age was, how sure we were of divine care. Amos took me by the arm and showed me the world, the palaces. I saw the palaces burning, I saw the world that had never been created. That famous first chapter of his, with its jokey, anxious, retributive structure, what is it but a theory of history as fratricide? Cain and Abel indeed whisper among the ruins, and Cain's mark is incised ever more deeply into his brow. No king could live except through violence, no one prosper but on the backs of others. For Amos, the very breath of the rich oppressed the poor. I have rarely met anyone with such a passion for justice. Justice, for him, meant a rethinking of the ethical and social foundations, a renunciation of violence, of the claims of oneself against another. He thought that everyone should be a prophet or Nazirite, that there should be no ordinary people, inhabiting, thoughtlessly, the social order. Where had he learned such hatred? Was it among the sheepfolds, the poorest of the poor? And when the Lord God called him, out of compassion, it would seem, bringing him to plead for his people, to the point of pity, was it just to dash him?

We were Judaeans, in a bewildering and demanding city. Amos was habituated to it, though always with an air of masquerade; even his accent shifted when he spoke to me, as if dialect were a sign of authenticity. We went to the taverns together; I well know what it is like to drink. You think prophets abhor drunkards; indeed, but drink gives joy to the heart, as you know, cools the tongue, makes life bearable. We prophets especially need to drink, to see, to listen, to the music that they played, there in the taverns. Death walks among the strings, and in the sweet wine. Uriahu himself never drank, and rather disapproved of us, the younger, more dissolute, generation. Though, goodness knows, Amos was his age. But Amos was different: outré, rakish, perhaps? Between us, there was a certain distance. It was, difficult as it is to admit, a matter of class. There must always be a suspicion attached to the propertied. I was living, more or less, on the labour of others. In Samaria, I stayed with Tyrian associates of our family friends. We drank their wine, and Amos was ever welcome, courteous, refined. One would never imagine that he disapproved of leisure.

He was a poet. Poetry brought us together. Language exploded between his teeth. Through poetry, we shared our visionary life. He understood the demands of metaphor, the terror of entering the inner chamber, the beauty of words, the hiddenness of speech. Any poet knew what he knew. There was an unexpectedness about him; as if the words relinquished their familiar territory, their markers. As if he had invented language. He stood in the clarity and emptiness in which I had nearly died. He is my guide, my alter ego, in the art of poetry; we are all his posterity. Epigones. Yet we are kin, twin; we share the voice, the intensity and freshness of perception. We knew ourselves to be the destroyers, and lovers, of the mortal, sowers of new worlds and language. I heard the word glittering on the Ionian sea.

As I wrote and rewrote my first vision, I realized that I was devising a new poetry. Slowly my voice, as I pared away the words, became pure, pure witness. Talia, and even my children, were in another world. Even Shear Yashuv, the child of convalescence. I sat at home, working, writing, the ghost of myself outside. From now on I live in a world of ghosts. I am a ghost. Amos was different, because he was solitary, unaccompanied by Uriahu, by Talia. In my voice you can hear them, the children, my vineyards, my intricate narratives, all those places to which I have been, all those people I have loved. Amos had been taken from the sycamore trees, and they spoke through him. And to tend the sycamores, those beautiful twisted trees, with their sharp and bitter leaves, their sour fruit, is that not a metaphor for attentiveness, as you pick the fruit before it is ripe, let it dry and sweeten?

The poem is so dark, so perfect—that three-part structure, that sense of dissolving syllogism. I wanted to describe the day of the Lord. The words fit into their places, bursting with life and rhythm. The logic is so sharp, so resolute in its march into nowhere. All that I saw, before I walked with

Uriahu into the inner chamber, before love, before humanity, it is all inscribed and spoken there. The world without God. The world without world.

I cannot describe darkness except through light. Erasure except through speech, repeating itself endlessly. Hence the parallelisms, one after the other, contracting to a point. And the point turns out to be no point at all. The bats fly in the twilight, the moles dig themselves burrows, the fellowship of worm and leafmould, and all is in an instant exposed, the limp trash of idols. The bats fly in search of the vanished caves. Like fish in air.

I wonder at my choice of words, so early, so long ago. I have been in so many bodies, inhabited so many words. I know what it is to be a young poet, I solicit the eager words, releasing them like bees from a calyx. And an old poet, for whom words are indistinguishable from memories, the care and protection of a grace, a gratitude, to invest, when we too become memory. The adventure, the risk, never ceases, never becomes easier. And so I found, as if full-grown, 'and with the children of strangers they clap', 'the delightful barques'. I found those strange obsessions and alliterations. I could turn things round and round.

And far away, the oaks of Bashan and the cedars of Lebanon, tall and lifted up, the high hills and rising summits, tower and wall, those couplings so easily made, interchangeable, I composed them, split them. To be so effortless, for just a few lines, to imagine the world and to take it away, in a breath, the thoughtless breath, that was something.

The line stretches to breaking: 'and upon all the cedars of Lebanon, high and lifted up'. And then it condenses into 'and upon all the high mountains', and the mountain turns into tower, ship and human being, and then the compact 'and the idols he shall altogether remove', comprising everything, all that clutter. The mountains with their calm wait there still; Lebanon and Bashan, with their forests, their cattle; ship and human being gazing with pleasure. I, exhausted, await the end, the day of the Lord, the interminable, which never comes.

The patience that I need, writing this, sitting still as a lizard, tongue hanging out, thirsty…the line, monumental, races to me, washes over me, that is what it is, an inundation. The line, so long, it could be the day of the Lord. The day of my birth.

The parable of the vineyard that you know, I discovered myself there also. It was by no means the first of my compositions. But it formulated for me, for the first time, what I was attempting. It was a parable of myself, and not as stereotyped, as simple, as you imagine. For it is I who sings. I sing the song for my beloved. I am the woman: Lilith, Asherah. I am the vineyard, I am the beloved, and I sing his song. We lie in the leaves, in the fragrance of the spring. We rise in the morning and go to the villages, and buy bread and milk at the creamery, and none looks askance, indeed they all love us. We stay at the inn of love, and for breakfast eat honey and sheep's cheese. Was it ever thus? I was always so decent. Will it be thus? Between Talia and I perhaps a prayer, a reminiscence, even without words. And God? The impenetrable, before childhood? So he longed, desired, walked in the world. And each leaf, frond, beckoned, love me, enter my portals, and each eye twisted in the wind. The lord of the world, in the silence, digs, weeds, clears stones, builds fences and towers. He wants a vineyard, his vineyard, scours me in his image. Every plant, every weed, cried; he cut the great trees. The animals cried, the mammoth, the lion, the soughing bear. He likes me, he longs for me, but I am not his. He went down to the nut garden to taste the precious fruits, to graze among the lilies.

Judge between me and my vineyard. What can the vineyard say in her defence? Nothing, my lord, nothing. Do with me as you will, open me, let the sheep plunder, the Assyrians. Let me lose your senses, your visage. Let the thorns imagine the roses, the wine pouring into cups.

The parable, so far away, the garden in which I sang. I could tell myself stories and read novels. I could sing to my beloved and call him to mind. And now, so far away, what is left to me, but this voice, this telling, when the towers fall, the bone ash gathers like an audience round my roots, and I cannot tell which is living and which is dead, which is cry and which is righteousness?

And it was in the year of the death of King Uzziah…you know the old king, the long years secluded in the free house, while the kingdom prospered around him. That infamous leprosy of his, red and white patches on the skin, would hardly have drawn any attention at all, if the king himself were not reclusive. There he was free of obligations; one visited him, out of necessity or friendship, accompanied by his books, his conversation. He was a charming old man. Ministers kept the requisite distance, while Jotham performed ceremonial functions. A satisfactory arrangement all round. I was not intimate with the king, though, as you know, my family had royal connections. Nevertheless, a great depression clung to the walls, the ravines, the Temple. It had been a long time since a king had died; it was as if something had died with him. I watched the funeral procession to the city of David. My reputation was growing; I gained in confidence. It is a slow and dangerous process, that acquisition. One needed a clientele, a readership, scribes, to be at the centre of a circle, inactive, attentive, without ambition. That was what I meant by purity. Between writing and speaking there was little difference. You think of us prophets as performers, and indeed we were good, on the whole, at the dramatic scene, but for the drama to be effective we needed the weight of experience, a constituency, you would say. A constituency without constitution. And so we were staying in Jerusalem, in Uriahu's house, sensitive to the least tremor. The sadness I felt, on the day of the funeral, was not just grief for a monarch, whose death perhaps symbolized the end of an era or a world, it was more personal. Something was impending within me, something had to be abandoned. The death was my death. King Uzziah's demise lingered on, like a malaise. The year of mourning, as if my tongue were coated with grime. Everything I said seemed to be tasteless, immaterial, hollowed out in advance.

And I saw my Lord, sitting on a high and uplifted throne…the Lord of all the earth, above temples, and mountains, and kingdoms, remote, inconceivable. There I was, the weight still dragging my heart, I had been to visit my friend the High Priest, we shared bread and olives, and we went into the Holy Place, the hekal, with its light shining through narrowing windows, the lampstand, the table, the incense altar, which had come down to us from Moses, cherubim staring at us from walls and curtains. I was so tired: the dilapidated house, patched and repaired through the centuries, through which glory seeped. A small golden chest, never opened, contained the petrified witness to God's word, inscribed with his writing, and there he spoke, between the cherubim, whose wings joined above: two inseparable for ever. Nowhere was holier, or emptier. A flask of manna, a rod with dried flowers, ancient almonds, gathered dust. Behind the curtain, heavy with the smoke of incense and viscous blood, crowded with barely stirring woven creatures, one could intimate the heart beneath the skin, but nothing was heard. I asked my friend what could account for this silence, this loneliness, in which we were, and he, who alone stood there, eternally, said that the fatigue, the utter listlessness, he endured perhaps meant that he could no longer bear the judgment on his breast. But what could have caused it? Uzziah was a good king, who did what was right in the eyes of the Lord—you can read that—and we suffered from no more than ordinary ills. I looked up, and there was the Lord. The Temple was open, the cedars were forests, mountains and rivers could be seen between the cracks. The Lord was waiting, a small smile on his face, as if a nut had broken open. It was not like the face I had seen in the inner chamber. It was much more terrifying. Perhaps because of the regalia. Perhaps because Uriahu was not with me. Out of the corners of his eyes came forth fire-creatures, and the resplendence filled the earth. His robes filled the Temple. One could not see for the drifting aurora. Above them stood the seraphim, their bodies incandescent, sheathed in wings, like a pupa in its floss. How many of them there were I do not know. One called to another, a solitary voice in all that confusion, the darkness formed between threads of light. For the first time I heard the three part Holy, the efflux of glory in all the earth. You have only heard it with human voices, indeed through my voice; but I heard it otherwise, in a language which will ever afterwards penetrate mine, turn it inside out, render it a facsimile. A language of such purity that no one can hear.

The walls and thresholds were shaking, and I too was shaking, from the immensity and fear of the voice, and the smoke rose and obscured the vision, and my eyes could not bear the glare and the incense, and I could not breathe. I felt the dishonesty of my lips, the coarseness of speech. All that I had written and spoken was dross, all that I had heard in his name passed through a sieve, until nothing was left. I was silenced, destroyed. I will die of vision. But one of the seraphim flew to me, and brushed my mouth with a live coal. Its iridescent body spun with heat, its wings enclose me. A spark enters my mouth, it is the holy seed, growing like a tree in my belly. It is very cold, like ice, round the wound, the seared flesh, and in my womb. I am Lilith, you know, and the seraph is the serpent. The coal comes from the altar, from the mountain of spices. The tongs glaze in the halflight, illumine each feather under the wings. It could be a nest. And then it pronounces its words of purgation, and I am released.

And I heard my Lord saying…his voice clear, sharp, I could hear it through my skin, my organs were transparent to it, I was all attention, upright, the wings still abruptly parting from me… I heard my Lord saying in the purity, and who indeed would go but I? So send me, send me, into the incomprehension, into the tarnished majesty.

I looked into the eyes of my Lord, and I heard the words that are on my heart and in my eyes and aching ears. To speak so as not to hear, to listen so as not to understand, to imagine so as not to see. Where weight and emptiness, vision and blindness, thought and clarity, are at odds, inventing always obstacles, to the immanence, the penetration. They are one now.

The human being, in what is it thought? In what it thinks? The thought, the high cirrus, blown by gusts to the end.

I turned and saw in my heart the folly and wretchedness, the pinches, the horrible pleasures, under the sun. You know my clichés: seek justice, do good. How can we return where we have never been? How can we be healed? To absolve the pride and beauty of humanity. And yet we desire to return with all our hearts, to undo all the hurts, all the wrongs. All that has been lost. The lost beloved. He wants and does not want. He invites and closes the door.

How long, my Lord?

I looked into his eyes and saw the desolate cities, the land without inhabitant. Where nothing reflects. Among the weeds, in the charnel house, a tenth returns, the holy seed.

GOMER'S REVENGE

Jonathan Magonet

At two o'clock in the morning, while my husband tossed restlessly in bed, I slipped downstairs and into the street. I knew the side alleys and avoided the watchmen as they did their rounds. They were always on the lookout for daughters of Jerusalem, wandering the streets, searching for their lovers. Once I too had had such romantic trysts, but then I was young and naive in the ways of men. Ivory limbs and necks of bronze no longer held much magic for me.

I knocked twice on the door of a small house on the outskirts of town and was admitted at once. The rest of the circle had already gathered and each greeted me with a hug or kiss: some with evident affection, others with a degree of formality I found disturbing.

Ruth called them to order at this bi-monthly meeting of the Women Against Patriarchy Consciousness Raising Committee:

'First let me welcome sisters from different lodges. It is marvellous to see mother Sarah of the League for Undervalued Matriarchs. It is a great honour for us that you have taken time from your Barren Wives Counselling Clinic to join us today.' A brief round of applause greeted this announcement, and Sarah bowed. If truth be told she was happy to get away for a while from the clinic. What with modern medicine, artificial insemination by donor, and surrogate motherhood, the clinic was going through one of its periodic bouts of soul-searching and reorganization. For example, should they extend their remit to include impotent fathers, or was that taking political correctness too far?

Glancing at the list in her hand, Ruth continued the welcome. 'Once again Huldah the prophetess has agreed to record the minutes.' Ruth smiled, signalling the usual joke. 'Of course, the good prophet that she is, she has actually written them in advance.' The women laughed politely but Miriam gave a frown. Since so few women were still allowed into the prophetic profession she saw nothing humorous in the situation. Her tambourine tinkled in her hand but no one else reacted.

Ruth continued with the list. Tirzah bat Zelophehad, representing the subcommittee on Biblical Law Reform, acknowledged the applause that greeted her name. On behalf of her sisters she gave a brief report on their negotiations with the Sanhedrin about maintenance rights for unmarried mothers. 'As things stand', she explained,

> the child follows the father in terms of rights and inheritance. So if the father is absent, the woman receives nothing. We propose creating a new system for the Jewish people whereby the child should follow the mother in all such matters. We call it the 'matrilineal line'. In this way we safeguard the rights of the child, and the mother will also be supported.

It seemed such a radical break with the whole of biblical tradition that most of the women were sceptical that it would ever be accepted. But the Zelophehad sisters had a number of major successes behind them, even winning over Moses on one occasion. So why not with this plan as well?

Ruth thanked them for the enormous amount of research and work they had done. Then it was my turn. Despite the warmth of Ruth's welcome I felt the hostility in the room. As the president of Adulteresses Anonymous, I knew that the other women, for all their liberal views and support, felt insecure in my presence. Inviting Ruth and Tamar to become honorary members and patrons of the AA had gone some way towards making the organization more acceptable. But for all their emancipation, and all their dislike of patriarchy, the sisters present still feared me and my members. The 'other woman' was still seen as a threat to the traditional family unit of a wife and two concubines. But what I wanted to discuss was too important to be set aside, and anyway it crossed all the divisions within the women's movement.

I was aware of a tense silence as I rose to speak. I myself felt uncomfortable. I had been so often treated as an object of someone else's actions or fantasies that I sometimes wondered if I had an identity of my own. No single word I said had ever been recorded in the Bible. How could I manage now in front of my peers?

'Sisters', I began, 'you all know me. I would like to pretend I am other than what I have been labelled. But by profession, at least, I am a harlot. That is how I earn my living. I could claim to have been driven to it out of financial necessity as indeed so many of my sisters have been. I could try to pretend that I am really a *kadeshah*, a Temple prostitute, part of the religious life of our community and simply serving the gods in my own special way. But that too would be false—even if some of my clients like to pretend that I am!' (I noticed that Tamar gave a little smile, and felt encouraged to continue.) 'I might even argue that I am really nothing more than an actress, playing a role in private that others do on a stage. And all of these things may be true at different times in my life. But, at least in the early days, I pursued my craft with a certain joy and enthusiasm. I enjoyed my sexuality. That what I did was clandestine and forbidden gave it an extra thrill.' I paused, and looked around the room, aware that everyone was paying close attention. 'And to tell the truth,' I continued, 'from time to time I felt a sense of triumph to satisfy a man who needed more than he could receive at home!'

At this an angry murmur broke out around the room and Ruth had to bang her gavel several times to restore order. When silence was regained, I continued, now unabashedly into my stride. 'I am sorry if that offends you, but amongst sisters, at least, we must be honest. I know that some of you were shocked when the son of Beeri asked me to marry him' (I could not bring myself yet to call him by his personal name). 'Well not as shocked as I was! At first I thought it was some kind of terrible joke. You know that prophets have the reputation for being crazy—present company excepted.' I smiled cautiously at Miriam and added 'at least male prophets. But he was persistent, quite urgent in fact and I did a quick calculation. I'm no longer young. I've only a few more years left in the profession—at least to make a reasonable living, so why not marry him, have children, settle down. And if from time to time I could see someone to make a bit of pocket money—well it would serve him right for picking someone like me in the first place. Well I won't bore you with the details. The beatings started soon after we were married but each time he would cry and apologize and tell me how much he really loved me. He was insanely jealous if I so much as looked at a man.

'In fact I tried to play straight with him—a covenant is a covenant. But he was obsessed. I thought he'd haul me up before the priest next to drink the waters of jealousy. To be honest I could even put up with his abuse. I've had it often enough before in the job.

'But something else is going on now. When he thinks I'm not around he gets out a parchment and starts writing things. Once I had a quick look. They are about me in a way, but being a prophet he managed to drag God in as well. I tell you the combination of prophet and prostitute, God and Israel, beatings and protestations of love is a terribly dangerous mixture. He's just waiting for us to have a child so that he can go public. That's why I wanted to speak to you. You all know how that business with the snake and mother Eve got out of hand. It took us centuries to get back some kind of equality with men. If the son of Beeri finds a publisher, it could all start up again—even worse than before. Everyone knew that Adam was none too bright and Eve was much more intelligent. But Hosea has God, the priests, the guild of prophets and half the men in the country on his side, and this time he's added violence to the mixture. So we've got to do something to stop him. A prophetic scroll like this could be all the excuse they need to lock us up, beat us, and maybe one day even burn us at the stake, all in the name of God.' I had a sudden feeling that I might have gone too far—the stereotypical hysterical woman—but I had to make them understand.

I stopped, quite exhausted, and looked around the room. Ruth smiled but the others could not meet my eyes. And I knew that I had failed. Even among my sisters some things could not yet be heard, especially when they came from someone like me. It was just too threatening for this time and place.

The meeting broke up a little later and I hurried through the streets as the first glint of dawn appeared. I felt quite sick and wondered if I had been so emotionally caught up that it had physically affected me. And then I remembered. Hosea had been watching me and keeping his distance, calculating that it was that time of the month. But there had been no show of blood. With a start of fear I realized that my warnings had come too late—it was all about to begin.

Hosea and Gomer Visit the Marriage Counsellor

Gillian Cooper and John Goldingay

Introduction

The book called Hosea gains much of its impact by beginning with third- and first-person accounts of the prophet's human love, which was an acted parable of Yahweh's relationship with Israel. Following the two accounts are prophetic sayings which explicitly portray that relationship in terms of a failed marriage, and subsequent chapters include further material which takes up the same motif. Then near the end the book includes another first-person passage in which Yahweh this time describes the relationship with Israel as that of a parent with children; it is again a troubled relationship.

The opening chapters of the book raise the problem that they describe events solely from the man's perspective, attribute the problems in the relationship entirely to female sexual faithlessness, support this stance by making Hosea symbolize loving Yahweh and Gomer faithless Israel, and portray Yahweh behaving violently towards Israel in punishment for her faithlessness. We are familiar with the experience of there being two sides to every marital story. We wonder what might be Gomer's. We are familiar with the problem that men may have with women's sexuality. We wonder in particular whether we need to ask questions about Hosea's explicit and implicit account of Gomer's promiscuity. We are familiar with violence as a feature of the marriage relationship, particularly when the man feels it is under strain. We wonder whether the attributing of quasi-marital violence to Yahweh reflects a feature of Hosea's marriage relationship, and fear lest it seem to offer justification for male violence within marriage.

It would be inappropriate to ricochet from a demonizing of Gomer to a demonizing of Hosea. We are also familiar with the way in which two people's description of their failed marriage can seem as incompatible as the marriage itself, and yet either of their descriptions can seem quite coherent and plausible when considered in isolation. One listens to a man or a woman and can imagine how they *would* see the story like that; one can feel the hurt yet have to remind oneself that both their interpretations of what has gone on cannot be true.

In this paper we want to try to imagine how Hosea and Gomer's marriage might have seemed to each of these people. We are utilizing what the book tells us about their relationship (our concern being the Hosea and Gomer portrayed in the book, rather than any 'historical' Hosea and Gomer who might be reconstructed: see Renaud 1983). We are utilizing what the book says about the relationship between Yahweh and Israel, on the assumption that this is also a prism through which their relationship is portrayed, and through which Hosea himself works out his difficulties. We are utilizing the 'gaps' in the story and seeking to fill them in the light of what is often true about human relationships, and of what we have ourselves experienced. Our aim is to get beneath the skin of Hosea and Gomer in order better to understand the prophecy of Hosea, better to understand the relationship between Yhwh and Israel which it portrays, and better to understand ourselves (see, e.g., Balz-Cochois 1982a: 41-42).

In our attempt to enter the text, we tried to imagine ourselves as Hosea and Gomer telling their story to a counsellor. After independently writing our separate accounts of their stories, we took part in an hour's role-play with a counsellor colleague. We then listened to a recording of the role-play and condensed the main points into a shorter dialogue in which Hosea and Gomer address each other.

In subsequently presenting this paper to the Nottingham Theological Society, we included a reading of much of Hosea 1–3. Several participants commented on the power of the material when read aloud. We ask readers themselves to read aloud what immediately follows, in a way which reflects the strength of the words, especially the violence and the yearning in the middle paragraphs. The notes relate only to some textual/exegetical issues raised by the material which relate to our particular angle of concern in this paper; many other exegetical points are of course debated.

Excerpts from Hosea 1–3

(1.2-9) The beginning of Yahweh's speaking through Hosea. Yahweh said to Hosea, 'Go and get yourself a licentious woman and children of licentiousness, because the land is rampantly licentious in its relationship

with Yahweh'.[1] *So he went and got Gomer bat-Diblayim.*[2] *She conceived and bore him a son. Yahweh said to him, 'Call him "God-sows"…'. She again conceived and bore a daughter.*[3] *He said to him, 'Call her "Uncared-for",*[4] *because I will no longer care for the house of Israel…'. She weaned*[5] *Uncared-for and conceived and bore a son. He said, 'Call him "Not-my-people", because you are not my people and I will not be yours.'*

(2.1-3 [EV 1.10–2.1]) But the number of the Israelites will be like the sand on the seashore which cannot be measured or counted. In the place where it used to be said to them 'You are not my people', it will be said to them 'You are children of the living God'… Say to your brothers 'My people' and to your sisters 'Cared-for'.

(2.4-9 [EV 2.2-7]) 'Confront your mother, confront her, because she is not my woman and I am not her man.[6] *She must remove her licentiousness*

1. '[Is] licentious/licentiousness' represent the verb *zanah* and a related noun which play a key role in this book. English versions translate by terms such as 'unfaithfulness' and 'adultery', but these are misleading. The words can refer to any form of sexual activity such as adultery, pre- and other extra-marital sex, incest, and prostitution, which take place outside social norms and thus constitute a threat to social norms. They need involve neither unfaithfulness nor adultery. They suggest female sexuality 'not subject to control' (so Setel 1986: 88; she is quoting from Dworkin 1981: 199-202; cf. Andersen and Freedman 1980: 157-63; Bird 1989). We accept the view that the book is not referring to any sexual rite; contrast, e.g., Wolff 1974 and Balz-Cochois 1982b; on which see esp. Keefe 1995: 76-89. A quite different counselling scene could be played out on the opposite assumption: cf. Balz-Cochois 1982a.

2. It would be too good to be true if the phrase *bat-diblayim* actually describes Gomer as a 'fruitcake' (see discussion in G.I. Davies 1992: 53).

3. The fact that she is not said to bear this child or the next child 'to him [Hosea]' is noteworthy.

4. Strictly the finite verb means 'she/it is not cared for'; the subject may be the land (v. 2).

5. Since breast-feeding inhibits conception, the mention of weaning here draws attention to its absence in the case of the previous child and underlines the hint that she was an 'accident'.

6. J.J. Schmitt (1989) notes that parallels elsewhere would suggest that the children's mother and Yahweh's wife is a city, presumably Samaria, rather than a people (cf., e.g., Isa. 49.14–50.3). In Hos. 1.2–2.3 (2.1) the implicit reference of the figure has moved between land, 'house', singular people, plural Israelites, brothers and sisters, and perhaps the city Jezreel; that flexibility suggests that reference to a mother city could at least be part of the picture subsequently in ch. 2.

from her face and her adultery[7] *from between her breasts.*[8] *Otherwise I will strip her naked and make her as bare as the day she was born. I will make her like the wilderness. I will turn her into a parched land. I will kill her with thirst. I will not care for her children, because they are the children of licentiousness, because their mother committed licentiousness. She acted shamefully when she conceived them, because she said "I will go after my lovers, who give me my food and my water, my wool and my linen, my oil and my drink". Because of that, here, I am putting a hedge around your way with thorn bushes, walling her in. She will not be able to go on her travels. She will chase after her lovers but not catch them. When she seeks them she will not find them. She will say "I will go back to my first man, because I was better off then than now."* '

(2.10-15 [EV 2.8-13]) 'She does not acknowledge that I am the one who gave her the grain and the new wine and the new oil and lavished silver and gold on her, which she used for the Lord.[9] *Because of that I will go back, and I will take my grain at its moment and my new wine at their time. I will remove my wool and my linen for the covering of her nakedness. I will now expose her stupidity before the eyes of her lovers. No one will remove her from my power... I will see to her for her days with the Lords for whom she burned incense and decked herself with her rings and her jewellery and went after her lovers—and forgot me'* (Yahweh's oracle)

(2.16-25 [EV 2.14-23]) 'Because of that I am enticing her and leading her into the wilderness and speaking words of love.[10] *I will give her her vineyards from there, and Trouble Valley as Hope's Door. She will celebrate*[11] *there in the way she did when she was young, when she came*

---

7.   'Adultery' corresponds to the verb *na'ap* and the related noun which denotes sexual relationships involving at least one person who is married to someone else. All 'adultery' involves 'licentiousness'; not all 'licentiousness' involves 'adultery'.

8.   The requirement to remove something from face and breasts may refer to adornments which Hosea sees as designed to allure: see the last sentence of the next paragraph.

9.   The word is *ba'al*, but this is its meaning; cf. 2.18-19 (16-17). The fact that Israel rarely called Yahweh 'Lord' is obscured by the substitution of the divine name by 'Lord' (or Lord) in modern bibles.

10.   Lit. 'speaking upon her heart'. On this phrase, see Landy 1995a: 50.

11.   We follow the Vulgate in understanding this as an occurrence of *'anah* IV (in BDB's categorization), not *'anah* I. In a context of grape-treading such as this, cf. Jer.

up from from the land of Egypt. That day' (Yahweh's oracle) 'you will call out "my man". You will no longer call me "my Lord". I will remove the names of the Lords from her lips... I will betroth you to me for ever. I will betroth you to me with right judgment and caring commitment. I will betroth you to me with faithfulness, and you will acknowledge Yahweh. That day I will celebrate'[12] *(Yahweh's oracle), 'I will celebrate the heavens and they will celebrate the earth and the earth will celebrate the grain and the grape and the olive and they will celebrate "God-sows". I will sow her for me in the land, and I will care for "Uncared-for" and say to "Not-my-people", "you are my people", and he will say, "my God"'.*

(3.1-5) Yahweh said to me, 'Go again and love[13] *a woman who is loved by someone else and who is an adulterer,*[14] *with love like Yahweh's for the Israelites—who turn to other gods and love raisin cakes'.*[15] *So I bought her for myself for fifteen silver shekels and a homer and a lethek of barley.*[16] *I said to her, 'You are to live as mine for a long time.*[17] *You are not to be*

25.30; and for women as the subject of this verb, 29.5, though in these latter two the verb is masculine. Exod. 15.21 is a less happy precedent from the exodus–Sinai narrative.

12. If the verb was *'anah* IV earlier, so it surely is here. The context is again harvesting, with Yahweh the subject, as at Jer. 25.30. For the transitive use, cf. Ps. 119.172. Of course Hosea did not have a lexicon to tell him that there were at least four homonyms of *'anah*, and the divisions could have been fuzzier for him than they are for us; to put it another way, paronomasia may be involved.

13. After the movement from *ba'li* to *'ishi* ('my master' to 'my man': 2.18 [16]), the movement from *laqah* to *'aheb* ('get' to 'love': cf. 1.3-4) is noteworthy, in the light of Setel's comments on the property implications of the first word of each pair: see Setel 1986: 89.

14. We have worked with the assumption that this is the same woman as in ch. 1; cf. e.g. Andersen and Freedman 1980: 291-94. A quite different counselling scenario could be played out on the opposite assumption.

15. As well as food used in religious meals (2 Sam. 6.18-19), these were apparently 'lovers' food' in some way: cf. Song 2.5. 'The Song of Songs is a...pervasive presence in this passage... The invective in Hosea is directed against a valorization of love and the world represented most comprehensively by the Song' (Landy 1995b: 153); he is actually referring to ch. 2. Cf. van Dijk-Hemmes 1989. Elsewhere—in implicit contrast to van Dijk-Hemmes—Landy also implies that Yahweh's 'romance'/'fantasy' in 2.16-25 (14-23) more positively mirrors the Song of Songs (see Landy 1995a: 49-50).

16. Both are considerable amounts, perhaps coming to the price of a slave, but we do not know why she needed a price to be paid.

17. Lit. 'many days', but the phrase surely suggests an indefinite period (cf. Gen.

licentious or to belong to another man. And I will also be yours'.[18]
Because the Israelites will live for a long time without king or commander,
without sacrifice or massebah, without ephod or teraphim. Later the
Israelites will turn and seek Yahweh their God and David their king. They
will tremble before Yahweh and his goodness in the end.[19]

Hosea's Account of his Relationship with Gomer

I was 22 before I married Gomer, rather older than the other young men in
the community. I had known many girls in our village and my parents had
discussed my marrying several, but they didn't impose a marriage to one
of them upon me, and for my part I couldn't be sure I wanted to commit
myself to one of them. Then I fell in love with Gomer, really, as she grew
up. As a teenager she had an animal sexuality about her, an incredible
physicality and liveliness. She was always unconsciously taunting the
village boys with her femininity. I realized I was wondering what went on
when they all went off walking and laughing and joking in the woods
around the village.

Being grown-up but unmarried, I didn't quite fit into village life, and I
suppose this was part of what drew me into serious involvement with the
shrine more than other young adults. I began to get angry with the way
most people in the village combined their allegiance to Yahweh with an
involvement in traditional religion. I wondered whether Yahweh wanted
me to speak out for him about this, but I didn't know how to do that; I had
no role models.

Then I believed that Yahweh was telling me to marry Gomer. I just
don't know how far I was providing a religious rationalization for what I
wanted to do anyway. I wasn't quite capable of thinking in these terms
then, but I have tried to since, though without coming to any conclusions. I
suppose I now assume that maybe both interpretations are true. I fancied

21.34; 37.34): cf. BDB 399b. Implicitly the phrase means permanently, as Hosea
hardly implies that she can resume promiscuity after a certain period.

18. It is usually assumed that these sentences imply a period of sexual abstinence
on the part of the couple, but this seems to be inference from what follows rather than
being required. As there is usually not a one-to-one correspondence between an oracle
or symbolic act and what it stands for, there seems no need to exegete these words
backwards.

19. We wonder if 'later' and 'in the end' are simultaneous with the 'long time' of
the previous sentence, rather than being subsequent upon it. Deprivation of massebah,
ephod and teraphim might well be designed to be permanent.

Gomer, she expressed all sorts of things which frightened me and also attracted me and which were what I might like to be but wasn't. I could fantasize about being married to her, but I might never have done it if I hadn't been able to tell myself that Yahweh wanted me to and that it somehow related to my growing conviction that Yahweh wanted something out of me. But I can't go back on the conviction that Yahweh really was involved with it all. So I believe Yahweh was working through my feebleness, my commitment anxiety, my fear and attraction, and my longings.

So I talked to my father about it, and he and my mother were only too relieved to arrange a marriage for me, I think, and we got married. And I loved her. I really did. I felt like someone who had been shepherding the sheep in the bare pasturage and was hungry and dry and suddenly found an oasis with vines full of grapes, or the way you feel when you have been looking forward to the fruit ripening and suddenly one day there are the first ripe tender figs on a virgin fig tree.

I'm not sure now whether she really loved me. I don't exactly doubt it. It's more that I came to realize more clearly how different she was from me, and I don't know how to think about what she felt. The difference was part of what had attracted me to her, but it became a barrier. She never thought the way I did, or reacted the way I did. If we had known about Myers-Briggs, we would have been able to discover that her profile was the exact opposite of mine. So she said she loved me, but love didn't cash out in the way I expected. For instance, I thought that when we got married, it would be her and me, together, the rest of the world shut out. You know, 'a man leaves his father and mother and cleaves to his wife and they both become one flesh'—not just in the sexual sense, but one life. But she didn't expect to give up her friends, all those young people with their jokiness and liveliness and their sexuality. I suppose I could have joined them all, but I didn't feel I'd fit. And by the time we had our first baby I was feeling resentful that she wasn't satisfied with me.

So I told her she had to stay at home with me. Then she would slip out when I was working or sleeping. So I would just pretend to be asleep and jump up when she tried to creep out and grab her and force her to stay home, or follow her and force her to come back home. Her loveliness still enchanted me, but somehow it became a distanced love, a love mixed with resentment and jealousy and anger and hatred.

Over three years we had three children. They were the children of closeness and distance, of love and resentment, of anger and hatred. I called them God-sows and Uncared-for and Unpeopled. They were theological names, names that reflected the stance I believed Yahweh took in relation to Israel. But they were names that spoke of violence and rejection and a broken relationship, and I knew that they reflected the feelings I had about Gomer.

She always said that none of those other young men meant anything to her. She said she loved me for the solidness and security and strength that I represented. But I never could understand why she wanted to spend all that time with them if they meant nothing to her. I used to imagine what they got up to. I challenged her about it. I said I knew she had affairs with them. I wasn't even sure that Uncared-for and Unpeopled were actually mine. I said I wanted to know what happened between her and those other men, but she refused to tell me. She wanted her own life as well as a life with me, she said. She didn't want to have to tell me everything about every relationship. I couldn't cope with that. I wanted to tell her everything about me (not that there was much to tell). I wanted us to be one, not separate people. As long as she wouldn't tell me, I could only suppose what went on.

I had vested my sense of identity in her somehow, and when she treated me as if I didn't exist—well, it was as if I didn't exist. I was more and more torn between love and anger, yearning and resentment. One half of me just wanted to punish her for causing me so much hurt, for behaving so unreasonably, for behaving as if she wasn't my wife and I wasn't her husband. The other half of me just wanted to have her back, longed for the fulfilment of the relationship that I dreamed of when we married. Sometimes I just wanted to hit her, and sometimes when it was a matter of forcing her back into the house or something of that kind, I wasn't sorry if her resistance led to her getting hurt. But sometimes I just wanted to whisk her away from all this, whisk her away from the village and the young men (and the young women who I suspected aided and abetted her) so that we could be on our own as I had dreamed we would be, so that we could start again and it would all be all right and we would live happily ever after and she would be mine and I would be hers.

That's still what I want really.

Gomer's Account of her Relationship with Hosea
Of course, that's just typical. It shows precisely what the problem is. It's all so rational, isn't it? Look at me, the great prophet, aren't I being entirely reasonable? No room for real feelings, no room for passion, and

no understanding at all of me and of what I've been through these last years. There's no talking to him, of course. He's got it all worked out in his head—what he wanted, what I wanted, how I went wrong. It's all a neat little package, which justifies everything he says and does.

There's the religion, of course: that's a big problem. He thinks I was the one who was unfaithful—what about him and his Yahweh? Just the two of us—but there are three of us in this relationship, and the other one is a very big presence. I've always known where I come in his priorities—a very poor second to Yahweh. How dare he pretend that I was everything to him? I've always known that when Yahweh called, he would go running.

There I am, stuck at home with the kids all day, and where's he? Out having meaningful religious experiences, or off preaching doom and gloom to anyone who'll listen. And then he has the nerve to try to stop me going out in the evenings. I tell you, he was unfaithful first. He was always first for me, no matter who my other friends were—and some of them were more lovers than friends, I admit it. I've never been first for him, though. Another woman—I could have dealt with that, you can fight another woman, you are on common ground then. But you can't compete with God.

So I not only have Hosea to contend with, there's his devotion to his God as well. Somehow he seems to imagine that our relationship has something to do with the fate of the nation —typical of a man to get these grandiose ideas about his own importance. At one time I could laugh at him; there was even a time when he could laugh at himself. I stopped laughing when the children were born. I don't know how I can ever forgive him for that. I mean, it was one thing to involve me in his vocation—I knew when I married him what I was taking on. I was an adult and I could cope. But when it came to involving the children—well, I don't know how he could. Our beautiful little girl, and he calls her 'Uncared-for'—what do you think that does to a child, to have a name that reminds her that her father doesn't love her?

Of course, he's not convinced he is her father. I suppose it's not surprising that he has doubts about me. I wasn't a virgin when we got married, and he knew it. Why else would I have married him? His parents were desperate to find him a wife. Most of the families in the village had already turned them down. He was so odd, you see. He would never join in village life, he was always on the edges. He was a pious boy, serious, boring most people said, but in any case just too odd. Parents of daughters want a nice normal boy for a husband, someone who can be relied on to provide for wife and family, settle down nicely to married life and fit into the community. Anyone could see that Hosea would never really fit in, and that any wife would have trouble with him. And the girls themselves, if they had any say, didn't want him—he was no fun, not like the other young men, joking and flirting and dropping hints of the delights of the marriage bed in store for us. Somehow with Hosea you just didn't get the impression of many delights in store.

And then there was me. I suppose he was my punishment really. I was wild. I could never quite bring myself to toe the line, to be the good girl my parents wanted. I was never quite satisfied with the conventions of life in the village. It seemed to me that there had to be more to life than a safe childhood, marriage to some boring man, one baby after another until I was too old, and a life of drudgery looking after them all. So I used to go out with a gang of friends, to the sanctuary mostly, to share in some of the wilder rituals there. And one thing led to another, and there came a night when I'd had just a bit too much wine, and the excitement got the better of me—and there I was, not a virgin any more. Of course word got out—you can't keep such things quiet in a small community like ours, especially when there is a young man keen to brag to his mates. My parents were desperate to marry me off then—when my father had finished beating me. There wasn't much by way of a dowry either—my father wasn't having the family money squandered on me after the way I behaved. There was some kind of financial deal behind the scenes, I think, and I'm sure my father wasn't worse off at the end of it. So that's how Hosea became my punishment. But I did try to make the best of it. And the children are his, I'm pretty sure.

We were two misfits, each disapproved of, each on the edge of respectability in the eyes of the community—but so different. We could have consoled each other, but that's not how it was. I resented giving up my freedom for the constraints of marriage and children. He came to love me, I think, or at least to desire me. But he never understood how to bring out the best in me, and because he didn't understand he tried to control.

So that's how the violence started. In that way he's so conventional, for one who's so unconventional about other things; he wants us to be like every other couple, husband in control, wife an obedient mouse. He just can't bear the thought that I have friends he doesn't know. He seems to expect me to cut myself off from my former life now that I'm married to him. But friends are important to me. He has his Vocation, and his relationship with Yahweh—but what do I have? Just him, and that's not enough. However much I loved him once, it was never enough. But he needs me there, doing as he says, agreeing with his every word. It isn't even that he wants me there physically, it's more than that, he wants me to be a shadow of him, hanging on his every word, totally devoted, with no mind of my own—like Israel should be with Yahweh, he says, whatever that means. And when he can't persuade me to toe the line, when his oh-so-rational arguments fail to work on me, then he finds other means of control. Violence isn't always physical, you know—though there has been the odd black eye. But there's always the threat, and there's the sarcasm, and the way he uses his words to make me feel small, and the way he constantly undermines my self-confidence and makes me feel powerless and useless. His talk strips me bare, and I think I can't take any more of it. But then he's sorry, and I just get a little glimpse of how it once was, and that makes me long for us to be able to work it out. The irony of it all is, I think he really loves me and wants me with him, but all he has done is to drive me away. The more he has blustered and threatened, the more I have needed my outings and my friends—without them I would have lost myself.

All I ever wanted was to be myself. He knew when he married me who I was. He was attracted to the aspects of my character he now wants to change. There's more to life than husband and children, and I want some of it. I haven't stopped being a woman just because I'm a wife and mother. I don't want to lose Hosea and the children, but I have to be me, and living with Hosea is making me lose sight of who I am. I know he wants me back. But it's no use pretending he can have me back where he wants me, that I can suddenly stop being sexual and become just a dutiful wife,[20] or that we can live out some kind of fantasy about just the two of us away from it all. When I got married, I wanted a lover not a lord and master, and I'm not going to change my mind about that. If we are to have a future together, perhaps I have to change a bit, but he has to change too. So long as he thinks he's God, it's just not going to work.

---

20. 'It is not sexuality that is the problem, but the fact that it is not directed towards the husband… The marital image draws on both marital bonding and conjugal anxiety, and encompasses both the beauty of the intimacy and mutuality between Israel-as-wife and God-as-husband and the terror of it' (Frymer-Kensky 1992: 151). (Earlier, 'the marriage that results between these two partners is intense and emotional; it is also…a punitive relationship' Frymer-Kensky 1992: 144.)

Hosea's First Response

I can see I ended up trying to constrain you, but I don't think that's where I started. You know that your freedom was part of what attracted me. And I can see why you think that the threat of violence was about, even when there hasn't been actual violence. But I'm not a violent man, you know that. It was you who said I had no passion. When I said 'I'm going to kill you', it was pain talking. I didn't mean it. We Middle-Eastern men talk that way, anyway. You know you shouldn't take it literally.

When I tried to win your love—well, that's what I did. I wasn't in a position to force you to love me. I won your love. You more or less said it yourself just now. I can see that if I thought that marriage made me your lord and master, my bluff has been called and you won't play the relationship that way. And so what I am trying to do now is win you again, trying to remind you of what it was like when we fell in love, daring you to believe that it might be like that again, that we could start again. You used to call me 'my man', and that's what I want. I don't want you to call me 'my master'.

And I don't believe Yahweh is in the business of control either. After all, the Deuteronomists keep telling us that the reason Yahweh fell in love with us was simply love for us. In Yahweh's case it was love that started it. And what Yahweh wants, too, is to be called 'my man', not 'my master'. There are lots of things Yahweh expects of us, but a lot of them are a kind of framework for our lives; that's why they tend to be 'You shall not's'. Positively what we then do is up to us. There's one basic thing that Yahweh wants and that's our real commitment to him and to no one else. And I'm sorry, love, that *is* something that I want too from you. I can see that there's a sense in which I ought to be prepared to let you be a free spirit, but somehow that has to combine with there being a kind of exclusive link between you and me. Marriage has to have an element of that, doesn't it?

But I don't feel as if there's a tension between being committed to Yahweh and me being committed to you or you to me. Why do they seem like rival commitments? You can surely be committed to the children and to me. Those aren't rival commitments. Why is my being committed to Yahweh a problem? But I can see that I hadn't left enough space in my life for you separate from Yahweh, or space in your life for you on your own—and for you and Yahweh separate from me, if you wanted any, for that matter. But Yahweh isn't in the business of controlling our every action.

Gomer's First Response

The kind of God you're describing now sounds more like the kind of God I could have dealings with. But the business about exclusive loyalty is still something I find difficult. Why does Yahweh, why do you, need exclusive loyalty? Can't you share? Is it your reputations you are worried about, what other people will say if they see that you can't control your wife?

And the demand for exclusive loyalty seems to carry a threat with it, the same threat from Yahweh as is there all the time between us. If you don't give me your exclusive loyalty I'll—what? cast you off? strip you naked? punish you? destroy you? There's a sense of foreboding all the time, the sense of someone watching, waiting for an excuse to condemn. It's so different from what I am used to. I go to the sanctuary and there I meet quite different gods, much more friendly gods, who bring rain and sun, who don't judge or condemn or lay down conditions, who don't demand exclusive loyalty. I know you say your Yahweh doesn't want to control people, but the trouble is that when you talk about him you so often make him sound angry and vengeful. I think sometimes that you are making God sound just like you as a way of justifying your attitude towards me. Or perhaps it's the other way round—you react to me in the way you do because of how you view God. It's as if this parable of yours becomes a neat package that you want me to fit into. Hosea = God, Gomer = Israel. And what you want to say to the nation spills over into how you behave towards me. But I won't fit into your package. I'm a person, not a piece in a neat pattern, and I resent being forced into the role of the one who is rebellious and sinful just because that suits the message of your preaching.

Hosea's Second Response

I don't think it's a package. It *is* a parable, like you said, or a metaphor. A metaphor's not supposed to tie things up and it's not supposed to be limiting. It's supposed to open up thought, not close it down. I don't think I've learned everything there is to know about God. I've listened in to what they say about the gods at the shrine and I can see that there are things there that are true about God, that must apply to Yahweh.[21] I'm always realizing new things about God. I think it's vital that Yahweh is One, but I don't think I've got Yahweh all buttoned up, and if Yahweh is the one God, there must always be more things to learn. Maybe when

---

21. Cf. Wacker 1995 and 1996; and for the view that in 14.9 (8) Hosea is appropriating Canaanite tree symbolism as he has earlier appropriated Canaanite sacred marriage symbolism, see also Day 1980.

Yahweh told me to marry you that was partly because I could learn things from you, too. You have certainly made me ask questions.[22] After all, it's hard to believe that Yahweh told me to love you just because you were going to provide some negative symbolism. There must have been something about the potential fruitfulness of the love relationship. I was very struck by what you said about you and the children.

Gomer's Second Response
Now, if your God felt about Israel the way I feel about my kids, that would make the whole thing very different. When you talk about Yahweh and Israel in relation to you and me, I can imagine the conditions attached to the relationship. But the thing that makes my relationship with the children so different is that there are no conditions. They will always be my children no matter what. That's why I find it so hard the way you've involved them in the trouble between us and in your message to Israel. They don't deserve those dreadful names, and no father should be able to call them that. I certainly couldn't ever call one of my children 'Un-cared-for'—to me they're all loved, without conditions. I'm not idealistic about it. I know there are times when they annoy me, when I just want to get away from them. I'm sure that there will be times when I look forward to them leaving home and getting out of my hair, but the bond is still there. It can't be broken. In fact, I know that the right thing to do is to let them grow up and leave home, and I know that means I have to let them become independent and make their own decisions. And I really fear for them, the things they may get mixed up in, the people they may hang around with. Most of the time I'd like to keep them at home where I can protect them. That wouldn't be right I know; I will have to let them go eventually. But that doesn't mean I can ever stop being their mother. Whatever happens in the future, I will still be their mother and they will still be my children, even if a time comes when they choose not to remember that.

Perhaps if Yahweh were like that—bound to his people like a parent, committed to them no matter what, torn apart inside like a mother is torn when her children do stupid and dangerous things—perhaps if Yahweh were like that, then I could understand your commitment to him because he would be a god worth being committed to. But I can't reconcile that with the idea of Yahweh casting Israel off, sending Israel out into the

22. See Janzen 1982. We picture Gomer/Israel stimulating all three of what she describes as Yahweh's 'existential questions' in Hos. 6.4-6; 8.5-6; 11.8-9, Gomer contributing especially directly to the first and last.

desert, and so on, which is the way you talk about him. After all, I thought the stories about the beginnings of our nation told of Yahweh's love, his promise of faithfulness and forgiveness, a guarantee that he would never cast us off. Is all that cancelled just because of a little dalliance with the gods of the land?

It's as if Yahweh has forgotten what it means to be in a relationship where there is give and take, and has started behaving like you, like an offended and jealous husband, and has decided now that all the initiative must be with him. It must be his decision all the time whether this is a moment of love or a moment of discipline—just like you are with me. For me with the children it's very different—I react to them, and pay them attention, and take them seriously as individuals with their own desires and needs. Perhaps if you spent more time being a father you might be able to find a different way of talking about Yahweh. And you never know, it might mean we could find a better way of living together, too.

Hosea's Third Response

I know what you say about you and the children is true. I've seen you with them. And it does fit with what I know of Yahweh. It fits what I was saying about control and freedom, doesn't it? We have to set some boundaries for the children, but it doesn't mean we want to control them.

I want to go back to what you said about me being so rational, that I have no passion. I half admit that. I know I live in my head a lot. That's part of what attracted me to you again, the fact that you were different, you were physically so alive, you acted first and asked questions afterwards, not like me. But wasn't that difference between us something that also attracted you to me? Isn't it the case that you used to love me because I was solid and dependable—and rational?

But I only half admit being all reason and no passion. I've tried to express myself rationally precisely because I'm turbulent with passion inside and I'm afraid of it, afraid of what might happen if I let it out, afraid of the love and the jealousy and the sadness and the anger. Those moments when I have tried to stop you going out and I have hurt you, I didn't want to, I was trying not to, but another bit of me did want to hurt you. I'm sorry. And I do believe that Yahweh is like me, or like both of us if you like, with all the complicated feelings that I have or that we have. Yahweh isn't cold and uninvolved and rational in that sense. Yahweh is full of love and passion and jealousy and hurt and anger.

I don't know how to handle the question whether Yahweh's relationship with us is conditional. I know it starts from love. Yahweh didn't love us because we had earned love. Yahweh just loved us. And Yahweh carries on loving us because that's Yahweh's nature. And that *is* like you and the children. But remember I have also heard you coming down on them like a ton of bricks, and you know the way you sometimes storm out to go and see one of your mates, and I bet they have sometimes wondered whether mother would come back, whether mother's love was conditional. It's the same as me. I can see I could have sounded as if I could give up on my love for you. Honestly, there have been times when I have wished I could. But I can't. That's why I still want us to find a way of starting again. But I can see I've spoken with two voices. And I suppose the fact that I can see that in myself, or rather feel it in myself, has made me project it onto God. Or is it the other way round? Or is it that that was part of what God wanted me to get out of all this, wanted us to get out of it. You see, I think Yahweh speaks with two voices.[23] You can't get away from the tension in connection with God or in connection with human relationships. I have stressed one side because that was what I was feeling, but also because that was the side Israel needed to hear, because that was where Israel was, but that was interwoven with my sense of not getting the response I hoped for from you.

Conclusion

We will let Hosea thus have the last word—it is, after all, his book, and in it Gomer of course has no words of her own. Part of what we have been doing is to externalize one of the voices in the text and to give it to Gomer. In the process, we came to see what could have been Gomer's distinctive contribution to Hosea's thought.[24] We found our way from the account of the marriage in Hosea 1–3, to the rather different account of the relationship between Yahweh and Israel in ch. 11:[25]

---

23. See the discussion in Unterman 1982. Unterman suggests that there are several ways of relating these in Hosea: repentance is necessary to avoid judgment, repentance is necessary before restoration, repentance is a part of restoration. It is not possible to make a pattern out of them. They reflect the prophet's 'inner turmoil'. He is 'caught on a tension wire between two poles' (549).

24. For a moment one of us misread the phrase *huerisches Weib*, a German equivalent of 'licentious woman', as if it read *heurisches Weib* ('heuristic woman': no doubt it would really have needed to be *heuristisches Weib*). For Hosea she *was* a 'heuristic woman', someone who made it possible for him to see things.

25. We here follow NEB, except for the change of 'Baalim' to 'Lords', without implying a commitment to all its philological and textual judgments.

When Israel was a boy, I loved him; I called my son out of Egypt; but the more I called, the further they went from me; they must needs sacrifice to the Lords and burn offerings before carved images. It was I who taught Ephraim to walk, I who had taken them in my arms; but they did not know that I harnessed them in leading-strings and led them with bonds of love—that I had lifted them like a little child to my cheek, that I had bent down to feed them. Back they shall go to Egypt, the Assyrian shall be their king; for they have refused to return to me. The sword shall be swung over their blood-spattered altars and put an end to their prattling priests and devour my people in return for all their schemings, bent on rebellion as they are. Though they call on their high god, even then he will not reinstate them. How can I give you up, Ephraim, how surrender you, Israel? How can I make you like Admah and treat you as Zeboyim? My heart is changed within me, my remorse kindles already. I will not let loose my fury, I will not turn round and destroy Ephraim; for I am God and not a man, the Holy one in your midst (11.1-9).

Since the Enlightenment, or at least since the nineteenth century, the aim of biblical interpretation has been to understand a biblical author in an objective way, and we believe in that task. At the same time, in recent years the awareness has developed that every attempt at interpretation reflects the concerns and the experience of the interpreters, whether they recognize this or not. For evidence one only needs to look at the differences in interpretation over the centuries (Paul at the hands of Augustine, and Martin Luther, and Karl Barth, and Martyn Lloyd Jones, and Tom Wright, for instance). So we have been trying to be self-conscious about that fact.

In interpreting Hosea, there are two ways in which we could have done that. We could have shrugged our shoulders about objectivity and simply used Hosea's words to mean what they might mean to us in Britain or the USA in our day in the light of who we are. Instead we have taken the second way; we have attempted to use our subjectivity as a way into the historical meaning of the text with a view to letting that historical meaning then speak to us. In the end, there is no way of knowing that we have succeeded in actually doing the second rather than unconsciously doing the first, but the second is at least worth aiming at. We have nothing to lose and may have something to gain. Indeed, we believe that the attempt has made us take seriously aspects of the text that historical criticism has missed or glossed over. We have noted, for instance, a number of exegetical points about chs. 1–3, as well as the fact that in 11.9 Yahweh claims that he is not 'a man', *'ish*. Commentators have either assumed or stated that the text really means that Yahweh is not human, *'adam*.

Gomer's perspective has made us take seriously the text's actual words at this point and link it to Yahweh's wanting to be Israel's 'man', her *'ish* rather than her master.[26]

We have presupposed that for all the cultural differences between men and women such as Hosea and Gomer and ourselves, and for all the social differences between eighth-century Israel (and the communities in which the material now in the book was further developed) and our early twenty-first century Western civilization, and for all the theological differences between Hosea's Yahweh and the God and Father of our Lord Jesus Christ, there is also a continuity between those human beings and us, those societies and us, and that God and ours. When we read the story in Hosea, however, initially we may find it difficult to recognize woman, man, and God. We have been seeking to imagine what Hosea, Gomer, and Yahweh could have been if we take the text seriously and also take seriously that conviction that Gomer and Hosea were people we could identify with, and Yahweh was a God to whom we could relate.

26. See Schüngel-Straumann 1986: 129-31 (ET 210-13); S. Kreuzer (1989: 126-27) has questioned this argument, but his re-examination of the use of *'ish* fails to prove his point. 'Male' rather than 'human' fits all the Hosean references (2.4, 9, 12, 18, [2, 7, 10, 16]; 3.3; 4.4; 6.9; 9.7; 11.9). The setting of Yahweh's not being *'ish* over against Yahweh's being 'holy one' in 11.9 is especially pointed precisely because *'adam* would fit well.

HAMAN THE VICTIM

Philip R. Davies

In Great Britain, we celebrate every year the execution of a certain Guy Fawkes, a member of a Catholic conspiracy against a Protestant king (the King James of the 'King James Bible' no less) to blow up the Houses of Parliament on the day of the royal visit. Every year on 5th November, the 'Gunpowder Plot' is commemorated with fireworks and the lighting of bonfires. A central feature of this carnival is the 'guy', an effigy made of stuffed clothing. Days before, children will parade their effigy and ask for 'a penny for the guy'. On the day, the effigy is burned on the bonfire.

Political correctness still has some way to go in Britain. The government is worried about the danger to people of fireworks, and bit by bit the restrictions on their sale are increasing. But no one cares about the rest. No one thinks that burning even an effigy of a human is bad for children; Catholics do not shun the event because the tradition stems from an outbreak of feeling against Catholics. Perhaps in some people's eyes it is even the Pope being burned on the pyre; there are plenty of parallels for this practice, even in recent times.

Of course, the carnival has deeper roots: Guy Fawkes was not burned: he was 'hung, drawn and quartered'. The fifth of November is soon after Halloween, too. Is the burning of the effigy something more atavistic, not too distant from the burning of witches, the annihilation of evil spirits? Or are we witnessing a relic of an ancient rite of human sacrifice to the sun in hope of reviving its declining power?

Does anyone care? Only the historian, the student of folklore. I wonder how many of the present generation of British schoolchildren even know the history of Guy Fawkes and the Gunpowder Plot of 1605?

The Jewish Guy Fawkes is called Haman. He is in some ways unluckier than his counterpart. His story is remembered every year at Purim. His memory will not blur. Like 5th November, the feast of Purim evokes dark themes, of jealousy, of genocide.

Here is another point of view. Another story.

The Jews here in Susa are celebrating already, waiting for the end of me. They rejoice at the death of the man they thought plotted to exterminate them, a man they clearly view as simply evil.[1] But I am not a plotter and no hater of Jews. My downfall is the achievement of a bitter, devious and twisted man who has played the genocide game and won. Who will now probably take my place, as he always wanted and planned. Even though I knew how dangerous he was, I thought I was being too clever for him, playing him at his own game, calling his bluff. But I lost; whether it was just bad luck or bad judgment or both I can't say. But his plan becomes clearer every time I think back over the events of recent weeks.

The whole thing was quite definitely a plot, carefully and maliciously worked out. What's more, I don't have the consolation of knowing that the truth will come out. The story that will be remembered will be *his* version, I'm sure of that; and it will be the last part of his plot against me to ensure that I am remembered forever as the villain, and he and that girl of his as heroes—not just in the eyes of the Jews (well, that's understandable, really) but of anyone else. But the hatred, the vanity, the deceit were not mine.

I really had nothing, ever, against Jews. But how easy it can be to turn a vendetta against one man into a war against his people. I used to have a few Jewish friends, which is how I was able to work out what Mardukai was up to (I don't think he realized that I knew all about 'Agag', for example). I don't have any now, of course. Mardukai has successfully infected all the Jews with his own hate. So here I am, not simply out-manoeuvred by someone more devious, which is often the fate of a courtier, but forever vilified. Facing death is something I can manage; facing an eternity as an object of hate and derision, not just an arch-villain but also a buffoon—that is much worse. Little hope, I suppose, that these lines will ever put the story straight. But they are some comfort to me, and to what will be left of my family, if they are allowed to read them.

The trouble, I suspect, started some years ago with another Jew, probably as ambitious as Mardukai, by the name of Belteshazzar. He too was one of the exiles from Judah brought over to Babylon by Nebuchadrezzar.

---

1.   A view perfectly summed up in Michael Fox's verdict: 'Devious though he is, Haman is allowed no mysteries. His motives, drives, and attitudes are transparent, his twisted soul laid bare to all. None of his motives are obscured, and little is left for the reader to wonder about. Evil, the author seems to say, is really quite simple and obvious, however sneaky the evil man may be and however subtle he may fancy himself' (Fox 1991: 178).

He too made it to the royal court and got himself into high political office. The Jews here are fond of telling stories about him, and he's already quite a legend (they call him Daniel, by the way). He was basically a mantic expert, but better than the locals (and in Babylon that's saying something!) But they also tell stories about how he survived being thrown into a furnace and into a lions' cage. Pure fiction no doubt—no one ever persecuted Jews here. But Belteshazzar was certainly a great success, and more than one ruler made use of his services.

Mardukai was a great admirer of Belteshazzar and so I asked one of my Jewish friends (I suppose I mean 'ex-friend' now) about the man. He told me some of the stories. One of Belteshazzar's predictions, which did not strike me when I first heard of it, has come back to mind more recently: after the Babylonians, he had said, there would be three more great empires, and the last one *would be a Jewish one*, one that would last for ever.[2] Now, this is the usual chauvinistic stuff, and pretty harmless, I'd have thought.[3] Why shouldn't everyone dream of world-domination once in while? Certainly, the Jews here don't take it seriously. Most of them have settled down well; very few have taken up the repeated offers to go back to Judah. They send money back there, but they're happier to live here. They take local names, do business,[4] and in general are integrated quite well. And why not? They are getting every opportunity. After all, dammit, they've even got a queen now!

Mardukai knows all these stories, of course. He's no good at predicting. But he'd like to be another Jewish high-flyer. A man with that amount of ambition would love to have stories told about him, to be remembered long after he's gone. And he's got where he wants. He learnt from the Belteshazzar stories how important it is to *get noticed* in the first place. And I'm sure he also got from these stories the idea of the Jews being persecuted. He certainly exploited that to good effect in my case!

2.   See Dan. 2.
3.   Though Josephus was very careful to conceal it from his own readers: 'And Daniel also revealed to the king the meaning of the stone, but I have not thought it proper to relate this, since I am expected to write of what is past and done, and not of what is to be; if, however, there is anyone who has so keen a desire for exact information that he will not stop short of inquiring more closely but wishes to learn more about the hidden things that are to come, let him take the trouble to read the book of Daniel, which he will find among the sacred writings' (*Ant.* 10.210, translated according to the Loeb edition).
4.   For a glimpse of Jewish commercial activity in the Eastern diaspora, see Zadok 1979. On the Murashu archive, see, conveniently, Stolper 1992.

So the first thing he needed to do was to get the king's attention. He used the one real asset he has—he's the guardian of this gorgeous young woman. After the Vashti affair I'm sure it was his idea to get Esther into the harem. He probably won't admit it,[5] but has she ever done *anything* without consulting him first? Well, I'm not sure about that seduction, but it fitted into the plan so well, I'm sure he would have approved even if he hadn't actually told her what to do. Mardukai's great luck was that the chief eunuch took a great liking to Esther. I don't *think* Mardukai bribed him, though I wouldn't put it past either of them, knowing them both as I do. Still, I'm not sure Mardukai really expected his Esther to be chosen by the king as a wife. Just her being in the harem gave him an excuse for hanging around outside, enquiring every day after his girl. I know she has always publicly denied her connection with Mardukai (no doubt on his orders), but she told Hegai straight away. How else was Mardukai allowed to get so close to the harem? You know how harems operate: male contact is strictly regulated, and all enquiries are treated with suspicion. You can get thrown in jail just for staring at the main door! Do you think any man can just wander up casually and ask about a particular girl? So of course the harem guards knew who he was. Hegai told me that he knew exactly who Mardukai was, and because Esther was his favourite he told the guards to let the man wander around outside on the pretext of asking how she was. So he sees the guards every day on his visits. He gets to know them, chats about his lovely girl, whatever. Picks up the gossip. He's on his way already. He's networking.

Esther must also have told the king straightaway that Mardukai was her guardian, because when she passed on the news of the plot *she did it in his name*! Imagine otherwise: 'And how do you know this man?' asks the king, frowning in a most worrying way...! Persian queens are not supposed to get secret messages from outsiders. She would have had to own up, wouldn't she? But of course she had told him. How else does Mardukai end up with a position at the court, as a minor official?[6] Yes, Esther turned out to be a gilt-edged investment for Mardukai. When she was chosen as a queen, he found himself on the inside.

So what about that plot he uncovered against the king? That was his

---

5. Est. 2.8 coyly states that 'Esther also was taken'. But that Mardukai prompted this seems a reasonable inference.

6. On the significance of the phrase 'sitting at the king's gate', see Fox 1991: 38-39 and sources cited there: it means 'holding a government office in the palace compound'.

next stroke of luck, which he exploited with is usual deviousness. How *did* he get to know what the two harem guards were up to? That never emerged.[7] The man certainly had a network already, and he knew much more of the gossip than he should have. My guess is that one of the guards outside Hegai's harem might have been a bit indiscreet. Mardukai always made it his business to network, and I'm sure he stored every bit of gossip that came to him. I am suspicious, though: if a minor official like him knew about this plot, surely everybody would have known? The king has almost as many spies in his own court as he has wives. Was there *really* a plot, then, I wonder? Mardukai certainly fabricated a lie about me, so maybe he had practised already on two others? Or am I being paranoid? They *were* found guilty after all. But when it comes to conspiracy against the king, you are always guilty until or unless proven innocent; you don't get the benefit of the doubt, do you?

You can take my word for it! As head of security, I know exactly where the interrogation cells are, and I know several methods for extracting confessions! I don't know the statistics, but I'll bet you very few people escape an accusation of plotting against the king. It's always better to be safe in these matters and quite apart from anything else, executing a few guards for conspiracy discourages others from misbehaving. These guys were doomed from the moment the king heard about them. I don't think they ever even knew who had told on them.

So I'm not too sure about this 'plot'. Inventing plots is a well-tried technique of court politics. And Mardukai is an accomplished court politician. But even if there was a plot, or at least an indiscreet remark, why did he do it? It wasn't in order to get rid of a rival (as it was in my case). Not to save Esther; the king's hundred-odd wives were not likely to be massacred. It must have been in order to curry more favour with the king—to get himself noticed a bit more. Now here's how clever the man is. He denies his connection with Esther publicly for a long time, even when everyone in the harem knows it. And he doesn't report this plot via the usual channels, doesn't talk to the head of security (my predecessor), or ask for an audience with the king himself. No, he sends a secret message (and how did he manage to do that, you may ask?) to his ward Esther who then tells the king. He doesn't make the accusation openly, doesn't want (yet) to be identified as the source of the information. He'll take the credit later when it suits him! It *was* after all, a bit risky to use her

---

7. Fox (1991: 40) rightly says 'All this is quite mysterious'.

as a channel; Xerxes might have been suspicious that one of his queens passed on something like this, even from her guardian. But that was the only way to protect himself from counter-measures in court. He was then still only a minor official. You can bet that before long someone would be likely to accuse *him*! So it's done very secretly, though Esther makes sure that the king knows the name of the loyal subject—and it goes in the books, as an investment for a rainy day in the near future.

I had no inkling at the time of any involvement of Mardukai. If I had, I might have been grateful to him, because the whole episode got me a big promotion. The king decided he needed a new head of security. Perhaps Mardukai thought he might get the job. On the other hand, such an appointment might have put the finger on him as being the informer. And he wasn't really experienced enough for the job anyway. He knew he needed to plot some more, bide his time. But of course he hated me. That became clear from the moment I took on this job.

Why? Why? I thought at first there must have been several different reasons, both personal and political.[8] It was possible, first of all, that he saw me as holding the job he ought to have had, as blocking his way to the top. I had to be put out of the way. I was an obstacle: I had high office. And perhaps there was a bit of envy in it after all. We both started off as outsiders in Persian society, but while he had achieved some minor recognition through patronage, he must have felt inferior to someone who got there through ability. But I came to realize that this, if part of his motivation, was rather insignificant. The compelling motivation for Mardukai's hatred of me was something deeper and darker. I'll come to that presently.

Whatever the reasons, or whenever they began to work in his mind, Mardukai exploited his hatred with the coolest cunning. He refused to offer me the usual salute when I passed. I might as well be honest and

---

8.   Levenson (1997: 13) comments of the story that 'the personal has become the political', which is typical of all court intrigues. But racial hatred is a syndrome in which the two are not so easily disentangled, since it overwrites the personal with a stereotype, and needs to invoke political (in the widest sense) reasons for behaviour that exhibits traits of *personal* dislike. The cliché 'Some of my best friends are Jews' as a defence against a charge of anti-semitism, implies a separation of the two areas, and that cliché's inversion into an ironic admission of anti-semitism shows that we do not accept that separation. The Haman story illustrates above all how Mardukai's hatred of Haman stems equally from personal and political motives that actually feed each other.

admit I have a certain vanity. But more than that, I was surprised at this show of disloyalty, because it could have been interpreted as disloyalty to the king. It was a dangerous tactic. And strange. The gesture of courtesy to a high official was no big deal, and certainly nothing at all to do with his being Jewish. I wasn't the only one who noticed it. There were general murmurs around about the strange behaviour. Maybe I should have done something about it then. But I am not *that* prickly. Frankly, I was waiting for some of the others to have a quiet word with him and, if necessary, get back to me. Well, 'quiet words' may well have been exchanged, and Mardukai was ready. He needed a reason for his behaviour that would vindicate him and put me in danger. And so he came up with the 'Agagite' story.

The move was brilliant. He managed to explain his aversion to me in a way that could arouse sympathy. He got the support of the Jewish community at the same time—which was important, because some of them were not too happy about his personal ambitions, and thought he had gone too far in getting his ward in the royal harem, a not very Jewish thing to do. They knew that he intended *himself* to be the main beneficiary of her elevation. But he also put me on the spot. He played the race card. More specifically, he played the anti-semitic card. He accused me of being a member of an anti-semitic nation. He implied that I would like to make Persia 'Jew-free'. The great plotter made out that I had a plot. Hating me, he implied that I hated him and all Jews. I didn't have to show any personal dislike for Jews; it was enough to fabricate an ancestry.

My family actually comes from Elam, where 'Agaga' is a well-known name.[9] It's not my own name, but early on in my career somehow it stuck as a nickname. It's the kind of name borne by peasant families, not by the aristocrats, and I suppose it was used to refer to my rather lowly origins. But it was meant rather affectionately, I think. Until Mardukai get hold of it. And then I became an 'Agagite'.

So let me tell you about the 'Agagites'. When Mardukai started referring to me as '*the* Agagite', and they asked him what he meant, at first he just smiled and said nothing. Then they started asking *me* who the 'Agagites' were. I had no idea, of course. So I asked one of my Jewish friends—the one who had told me about Belteshazzar, in fact. When I mentioned 'Agagite' to him he froze. But I got the story from him in the end. And it is quite a story!

9. See Zadok 1984: 18-23.

First of all, then, there is a Jewish tale of a king called Agag, a ruler of a people called the 'Amalekites', whom their first king (called Saul) was ordered to kill. Saul was ordered to wipe them out, and here is how the command was translated for me:

> Go and attack Amalek, and wipe out all their property. Don't spare any of them—kill men, women, children, babies, as well as cattle, sheep, camels and donkeys.[10]

Read that carefully! Who is going to attack whom here? Who starts the trouble?

Anyway, poor Agag, though spared by Saul (whom the Jews have mixed feelings about!) was finally cut to pieces by a Jewish holy man. I was rather upset to learn that 'Agag' meant an enemy of Jews. I prompted my Jewish friend for more information. With some reluctance, I got a lot more out of him. For a start, there's a law in one of their holy books that commands all Amalekites to be exterminated. I'll give you chapter and verse again, as translated for me:

> Remember what the Amalekites did to you on your route out of Egypt, how they met you on your march, and killed the stragglers, all those who were weak, at the end of your line when you were all vulnerable and weary. So, when your god Yahweh has given you respite from all the enemies around you, in the land your god Yahweh is going to give you for your possession, blot out the memory of Amalek from the earth. Do not forget to do this.[11]

Well, I thought it seemed rather a harsh response to the incident. In the desert we all survive by raiding each other. The resources are pretty scarce there, and you need to protect your territory. A large armed force marching through is an obvious threat—and an obvious target. The Amalekites must have been heavily outnumbered and so they attacked from the rear, picking off the weakest. Not very nice, I'll admit, but not exceptional. Hardly a reason to hate Amalekites so much and want to exterminate them. Given all the wars between the people in this world, if everyone felt that way, there'd be none of us left.

So I naturally asked to hear the story about this raid on the Jews coming from Egypt. Then came the surprise: *there is no story*! The Jews pride themselves on having ancient records of their history back to this country itself (they claim their ancestor was called Abraham and came from Ur in

---

10. 1 Sam. 15.3.
11. Deut. 25.17-19.

Babylonia[12]). But there is no story about this raid. What there is is a story about an *attack on Amalekites*. You must listen to this. Here again is the translation I was given (Moses is their great leader and lawgiver and Joshua is his deputy):

> Moses said to Joshua, 'Choose some men, and go out, fight with the Amalekites: to morrow I will stand on the top of the hill with the "rod of God" in my hand'. So Joshua did as Moses had told him, and fought with the Amalekites, while Moses, Aaron [that's his brother], and Hur went up to the top of the hill. And when Moses held up his hand, Israel got the upper hand, and when he let down his hand, Amalek did better. But Moses' hands grew heavy; and so they took a stone, and put it under him, and he sat on it; and Aaron and Hur held up his hands, one man on each side; and his hands were steady until sunset. So Joshua put the Amalekites to the sword. And Yahweh said to Moses, 'Write this down in a scroll as a record, and repeat it verbally to Joshua: I will blot out the memory of Amalek from the earth'.[13]

Can you see it now? *That's* where the law originally came from. Not from an Amalekite attack, but from the Jews! They went after these Amalekites and then decided they would blot them out. I have to tell you, even my Jewish friend was surprised. He knows his traditional literature as well as most educated Jews, but he's always assumed the Amalekites started the trouble. Of course, he imagined that the Amalekites *had* done something bad first. But he had to admit that this was not recorded.

Did Mardukai expect I would discover the truth? That it is the Jews who hate Amalekites and not the other way round? That this hatred is unprovoked? That these Amalekites have always been the victims? And what would I learn from my researches? To start hating Jews for the way they behave? To start identifying with these poor people and their wretched king, 'Agag'? Well, I have to say, I did find my attitude towards Jews changing. It shouldn't have. I am sure these are ancient legends. I am sure no Jew goes round looking for Amalekites to exterminate. I am sure no Jews would recognize an Amalekite if he saw one!

But *one* Jew does. He pins the label 'Agagite' on me, and the old stories of racial hatred begin their insidious work. On both sides. Jews begin to hate me. I begin to hate them. Mardukai waits for his own advancement. Brilliant. Like the ancient Amalekites, I am the victim of hatred but am going to be blamed. I am going to have hatred pinned on me.

---

12. Gen. 11.31.
13. Exod. 17.9-14.

But my researches showed me something more, of course. It's now time to reveal Mardukai's hidden motivation for his hatred of me. In the hope of discovering some reason for his hatred, I had tried to find out what I could about him. It did occur to me that I had in some way offended or even injured him in the past. Maybe there could still be a reconciliation? I doubted it, but I was curious nevertheless. And then I came upon it. There was one thing that every Jew, it seems, knew about Mardukai, because he was especially proud of it. He came from a Jewish tribe called Benjamin. This was apparently unusual, since most Jews were from Judah (as the name implies). But more than that: he claimed to be descended from the first king of the Jews, who was also from Benjamin. That king was Saul![14] Saul had waged war on the Amalekites, and his disgrace had begun when he failed to execute their king. As a result, he lost the favour of his god and was killed (with his sons) in battle, his body exposed on the walls of a Philistine city.

That shame must be something Mardukai still felt as he continued to claim the nobility of his descent. And now he was determined to avenge the reputation of that line. There were no Amalekites left for him to vent his hatred on, but he had now managed to invent one, someone he already had a personal reason to hate. There is a deep psychological sickness in this man, and he saw in me a remedy for it. If he carried the shame of Saul with him, my nickname 'Agagi' must have hit him hard when he first heard it—and then he saw a means to turn it to his advantage, heal his sickness, and remove a rival.

I felt both relieved and alarmed when I discovered this. I was relieved to discover that Mardukai's hatred for me had nothing to do with my own faults, but with his. At least I knew what I was facing. But I also realized that a hatred with such deep roots and embedded in such a devious psyche would not be abandoned by any persuasion, by any attempts at reconciliation. It was likely that if he had not, then he soon would really identify me in his sick mind as a reincarnation of the old enemy of the line of Kish, as Agag *redivivus*. So no matter that there is not even such a thing as an 'Agagite'!

I learnt later that Mardukai twisted the knife a bit further into me. There is also a prophecy from one of the Jewish mantics called Ezekiel who was

---

14. See Est. 2.5, which also mentions the Judaean king in the same sentence. It seems probable that the reader is meant to note that *two* royal lines were carried off into captivity together. For comment on Mordecai's descent, see Levenson 1997: 56 and Laniak 1998: 66.

a contemporary of Belteshazzar's and was actually brought in the same group from Palestine to Babylonia. In his prophecy the Jews will return to their land, and then they will be attacked by a king called 'Gog'.[15] Well, this was a pretty obscure and rather fanciful piece of ranting, but everyone knows about it now. Mardukai has been putting it about that Gog is 'Agag'[16] and that he is an Amalekite. So every Jew is becoming convinced that I am a sort of 'Gog' who wants to wipe them out and who (so the prophecy says) will be wiped out himself by their God.

That's what they will be thinking when they see me on the gallows tomorrow. And the last thing I shall probably see is the smile on Mardukai's face. He's got what he wanted. And remember the words 'blot out the memory of Amalek from the earth'? Well, they're getting fulfilled. But to do all this he had to stir up something that may well go on for centuries. Racial hatred is hard to eradicate. It's a dangerous card to play. I am the so-called 'enemy of the Jews' now. But some time, it might turn on the Jews themselves. For there will always be people looking for a scapegoat. All you need is some old legend, some remembered insult or crime, and people can quickly learn to hate an entire race. If ever the Jews are unlucky enough to be accused of some crime, from an individual murder to an international conspiracy, they will surely know how I feel and what I am suffering. Even in this most enlightened of empires, it's happened. I'm not sure myself if I hate Jews a bit already. Maybe I am beginning to. I can certainly see how easy it is to stir up these feelings that I never had before. That's what Mardukai may have done to me, just as he has done it to his own people.

Was I at all to blame? Probably. Had I known, I could have acted differently. I fell into his trap, thinking that I was being clever. I decided I could play the same card; beat him with his own weapon. If I am supposed to be a member of an anti-Jewish race, I'll show him. Now, of course, he will claim that this is where it started![17] Just as the Amalekites were supposed to have started their feud. I did something very unwise: I went to the king and suggested that there should be a decree for the destruction of the Jews. Of course, I didn't set it in motion immediately. I proposed a deadline, a very safe one. I went to the king in the first month, and the deadline was nearly a whole year later, midway through the twelfth month. It was, I thought, a clever ploy. First, it would give the Jews plenty of time

15. See Ezek. 38–39.
16. See Fretz 1992.
17. And indeed, this is what Est. 3.6 does say!

to put some pressure on Mardukai to do something about it. He would surely like that, I reasoned: he could be the saviour of the Jews. All he had to do was deal with me. I knew he would hate that, but I wanted him to see who really had the power, and I wanted him to see what kind of game he might be playing with his racial card. I believed, stupidly, that he was amenable to reason, or a least to a dose of political realism.

I was also careful in how I had the decree worded. I made the basis of the charge that the Jews did not obey the king's laws. That way, I could be sure the king would agree, and that way, I thought, most Jews would get away with it, because to my knowledge they are a very law-abiding people and don't cause trouble. I wonder if Mardukai realized where I got this idea from? It was from the stories of Belteshazzar. In one of the stories, the king (it was Darius, though by then Belteshazzar was supposed to be dead!) was asked to issue an edict against anyone who would not pray to the king himself (another silly idea: no one prays to the king!). The point about this story is that it wasn't really aimed at the Jews, but was a plot to *get at Belteshazzar himself.* He's the one they wanted. In the same way, Mardukai was my target. I was giving him a year to wriggle uncomfortably, and to come to his senses. The nice point was that in refusing to bow to me he was technically refusing to bow to the king, and so my proposed decree could indeed be said to be targetted at him personally.

He would know what I was doing. I had the decree worded to include all Jews, men, women and children, deliberately echoing the fate of the Amalekites. Mardukai would understand. But did I make a mistake in not telling the king what this was all about? He might not have agreed: he might have resented being manipulated into what he could have seen as a private feud. And of course, this woman Esther was around. Did he realize she was Jewish? I really don't know. Why should she have told him? And even if she had, she clearly was not behaving as Jews were described in the decree. If she was a queen, she'd hardly be guilty of not obeying the royal laws!

But I made a fatal mistake. Unlike Mardukai, I was allowing my heart to rule my head. I wanted revenge on him, I wanted him put in his place. Did I also mind if the Jews were frightened? Well, I suppose I did think about that, but not too much. Maybe they deserved to live for a day or two with the threat of being treated as they had treated the Amalekites, even if none of us believed the old stories. Yes, I think maybe I was already showng some (small) signs of that racial disease that Mardukai was infected with. I mean, Mardukai had not personally invented their hatred against the

Amalekites. That was already in their writings. So maybe they would now see what such attitudes could lead to. A short dose would not do them any harm. But of course, it always does. Humans still have this to learn. Racialism is a virus.

Mardukai was too good a schemer for me. I tried my hand at the game, but he was a master. Of course he didn't react as I had hoped. Far from trying to stop my little ploy, he did just the opposite. He immediately dramatized the whole thing, put on mourning clothes, paraded up and down. More importantly, he again enlisted Esther in his dealings. Just as he had with the 'plot', he used her as the vehicle of communication with the king. She was reluctant this time, I know, and apparently gave some excuse about not being allowed to approach the king unbeckoned. She was trying to say to him, I think, that the honeymoon with the king was over and now she'd have to wait her turn for the royal bed like all the rest. At this point I am sure she knew what Mardukai was up to, and wanted to be involved no further. Very sensible, that. The king can divorce as well as marry! And where would that have left Mardukai? But he had no choice, did he? In the end, she agreed. She was still a pawn.

But what was the move? To plead on behalf of the Jews? Own up that she was one of them and they were really nice people? If the king had decided to interview me about this I would have had an answer ready. I would have explained exactly what game I was up to. I wouldn't be surprised if Esther herself had an inkling of what it was all about. But she wasn't giving the orders, although Mardukai always claimed that he was pulling no strings at all with her (which, given she was the queen, was the obviously safe thing to say, anyway). No, no, no! Esther wasn't worried about the Jews—not yet, anyway. Nor, of course, was Mardukai. The decree could wait (remember, he had a whole year to work on that!); meanwhile, he wanted to be rid of me first. At least that proved I was right about him: he was more obsessed with his hatred of me than he was about the fate of his people!

I'm still not sure what his plan was, exactly. I was to be invited to a dinner party with Esther and the king, that's clear.[18] I guessed at the time, unaware of what was really being plotted, that some kind of deal was going to be offered to me to revoke the decree in some way in return for…what? I assumed that Esther was instructed to be Mardukai's intermediary, which would at least save him from having to talk to me himself. A pity that Mardukai could not bring himself to surrender in

---

18. The biblical text is in confusion about two banquets; see Est. 5.1-8.

person, but had his girl do it. Still, I would have to accept that. He, meanwhile, was still in his usual position that day, ostentatiously exempting himself from the general salutes when I passed. At the time I wondered whether he really knew about Esther's initiative, and whether he'd be so arrogant afterwards when he learnt the conditions I would put upon any deal. I still didn't realize at that time that he was carefully orchestrating my own destruction. To be fair, I don't think even Esther knew at that stage what he had in mind.

I was too nervous and excited that evening to worry about my persecutor. A private dinner party with the king certainly meant I was in favour: maybe promotion, a gift or two? I was also looking forward to meeting this Esther in person for the first time. Was she really Mardukai's pawn, I wondered? Did she feel like him, or was she herself aware of his 'problem'? Maybe I could even get her to tell me more about him.

I was out with some friends that evening. I did drink a bit too much, I know, and was talking a lot about what the king might have in store for me. I also went on a bit about Mardukai. But none of them had any explanation. However, they wound me up. They pointed out that refusing to salute me, although irritating more than anything else, constituted adequate grounds for suspecting his loyalty to the king. Why didn't I have him arrested and executed straight away? I had toyed with such an idea before, but it seemed a rather excessive measure, and anyway I was not too sure of the king's attitude towards him, or indeed whether executing someone who was almost a father-in-law might not displease him. But now that I knew I was in the king's favour, I could risk it. Of course I was not going to do anything until I had seen the outcome of the dinner party, but a little preparation would do no harm, and if I could put it around that the intended target was Mardukai, I could at least wipe the smirk off his face. If I made sure the news got back to Esther in time, it would also give me an extra bargaining chip if I needed it. I would of course reprieve him, with a great show of reluctance, and on condition he showed no more signs of insubordination and publicly acknowledged my status.

So I iced the cake. But these gallows were a fatal error of mine. With hindsight I can see that they were born of passion more than reason. Had I really wanted to be rid of him, I could have had Mardukai quietly beheaded or strangled. But the threat of a public display satisfied me more. That, I was told, is how Saul had ended up, dangling from the walls of a city.[19] Mardukai would surely not be able to bear the thought of repeating

19. 1 Sam. 31.10. See also Laniak 1998: 68 n. 80.

the fate of his ancestor. I made the analogy very clear by ordering that the gallows should be constructed as high as possible, so that they could be seen from the whole city.

The news reached Esther for sure, and quickly. And my grim little joke misfired. Her plan (Mardukai's?) must originally have been some kind of cosy compromise before the king and me, with her admitting that she herself was Jewish and asking for the decree to be revoked. Caught between her charm and my own evident loyalty and efficiency, the king would give in to her and compensate me with some reward. But now she would have to change her ploy and plead for Mardukai. Mardukai was a silly and bitter man, she would say, but not disloyal to the king; she would ask him, and he would ask me, to reconsider. I would have to express my zeal for disciplining all those posing any threat to the king (I would remind him, and her, of the decree against the Jews at this point) but would accept the king's command. We would then do the original deal over the Jews and in return for some further signs of royal favour I would accept the outcome. Far too complicated! Why didn't I just leave out the gallows ploy? I know that I did it out of a desire to terrify Mardukai personally. But it was a tactical error: Esther, up to this point perhaps no party to Mardukai's plot, might now turn against me. And she did.

The dinner party was, of course, a disaster. First, the girl didn't just go and *see* the king. She stayed the night. And she planned his bedtime reading. Had Mardukai instructed her what to do? Probably: but she was certainly bright (and now motivated) enough to have contrived this herself. Xerxes was in the habit, as everyone in the palace knew, of reading about himself. He liked to check upon the annals now and then, and often he dictated some amendments. She must have talked to him, casually of course, about the new gallows and the hanging planned for tomorrow before she retired. And somehow arranged for a particular set of annals to be brought if he asked for them. As he did. And while Esther no doubt kept her fingers crossed back in the harem, the king read about the plot and recognized the name of the informer.

So that part of my plan was undone before the dinner party started. At the very least, Mardukai was not going to have to grovel. I was not going to hang him. But we could still negotiate about the Jews. This was my thinking at the time. So next morning, well before the dinner party, I was summoned to the king's presence and was surprised to be offered any kind of gift I wanted there and then. I just had to name it! I was really quite unprepared—I'd hoped for something at the dinner party, but not such a public offer here and now. So I stammered out whatever I could think of, which, bearing in mind what I could have asked for, was something stupid like a royal procession. All I could think about was Mardukai, and I wanted something that would demonstrate my complete victory over him, force him into public submission.

I had no idea, of course, about Esther's little ploy. When he gave the order for Mardukai to be treated this way, I quickly recalled what the king had *really said*, the words which I had not properly taken in. 'What should I do', he said, 'to the man I wish to honour?'—looking straight at me. Was it a trick question? I still don't know. Perhaps my fate was already sealed, if the king knew I intended to hang the man whom he believed had saved him from assassination.

My friends had no doubt. They advised me to be very careful indeed. I was not only up against Mardukai, but also his accomplice, Esther, and quite possible by now the king himself! They were worried for me. They could see, even more clearly than I could at the time, how precarious my position was. But what could I do? So long as the king retained me in my position, I was safe. But was Mardukai satisfied with his victory? Clearly not. Once the procession was over, he returned to his position. While his hero, Belteshazzar, had been promoted to the highest office below the king, he had not. I was still in my post. And the edict against the Jews stood. Perhaps, after all, I had not lost yet. The dinner party that evening would determine who won.

It was a long dinner party, not unusual with the king. But the longer it went on the worse I felt, and not because of the wine! I felt the whole thing was a game—worse, a trap. Finally, as if in a rehearsed move, the king turns to Esther and says, 'Well, my dear, so let me ask you again: what would you like? Up to half my kingdom!'[20] And she had her answer well-rehearsed, word-perfect. How she would like the lives of her people. She piled it on: her people had not merely been sold, they were to be destroyed, and she finished off by pointing out how valuable the Jews were to the king, and how he could never be compensated for their loss. 'And who', says the king in what I know is mock surprise, 'is responsible for this?' He knows well, of course, because he had signed the decree himself only a few days earlier!

So my fate has been sealed before the party begins. I wait for the king to turn on me. But he doesn't. Feigning anger, he simply leaves. He leaves me alone with Esther. The game, evidently, is not over. Is there, after all, a

---

20. This was a common royal idiom, meaning, 'anything within reason'.

reprieve? Have I already been taught my lesson? Or is the knife to be twisted further? Whatever the planned outcome, the endgame is to be played between the two of us. What move am I supposed to make?

I don't have any cards left. Except that I am still here, and so is she. Perhaps I am now supposed to beg her to intercede for me. But first I need to find out the truth. Why does Mardukai hate me? She gazes uncomprehendingly at me. I invent the words for her: why shouldn't he hate me? I am a Jew-hater, an Agagite. I try to explain that I'm not, that it is Jews who hate Agagites anyway, and no, that actually, it is about one Jew hating one Agagite who isn't even an Agagite because there are no Agagites. I stumble on, half-drunk and in a state of near-panic. I try to explain why I had that decree issued, how I was driven by Mardukai's hatred and blunt refusal to acknowledge me, driven to this stratagem.

She keeps filling my glass. Her face is blank, stony. She can only repeat 'you want to kill us all'. Is she really stupid? Can't she understand? Has Mardukai brainwashed her? Does she, too, have something personal against me, beyond the gallows being constructed for her guardian?[21] I feel myself almost turning into an Agagite, confronted by an irrational, stubborn, vindictive hatred. We have each drunk Mardukai's poison, and are learning to hate each other.

> Blot out the memory of Amalek from the earth. *Do not forget to do this.*

She has not forgotten. There is a principle that the law of the Persians can't be revoked.[22] The law of the Jewish god is obviously just the same. Forgiving and forgetting are not allowed.

The final move. She smiles. 'Will you beg me to help you out?' she asks. In a state of near-drunken exhaustion, with defeat the only taste in my mouth, I caught what might have been the lifeline. I bend over in front of her to kneel on the floor, and collapsed in her lap. Right on cue, the king returns (from where he has been watching?). He calls the guards and I am dragged off. The last thing I hear is the king shouting 'assault', 'rape' and the last thing I see is Esther's smiling face. A smile of triumph, pleasure and, I think, of everlasting hatred.

---

21. Timothy Beal (1997: 96-106) highlights the theme of 'coming out' especially in relation to Esther. If Haman was looking for an additional reason why Esther should hate him, it is perhaps that his actions forced her to 'come out'. If so, then it is ironic that she should now seek to rescue those from whom she previously preferred to dissociate herself. Beal's suggestion is attractive but leads to disturbing implications. Was Esther's resentment, then, really at being Jewish? Was Haman the target of a *self*-hate?

22. See Est. 8.8.

'Bring Agag, king of the Amalekites to me'. And Agag came to him hesitantly.[23] He said to himself, 'Surely the taste of death has gone?' But Samuel said, 'As your sword has made women childless, so shall your mother be childless among women.' And Samuel hewed Agag into pieces before Yahweh in Gilgal.[24]

I have written a note to my wife and sons. They had better believe me, they are in trouble. They are 'Agagites' too. So far Mardukai's hatred has known no boundaries. Will he stop now? I've told them to leave as quickly as they can. I only hope they'll believe me. I can't predict what will happen next, but I don't think this business is over.[25]

Kill men, women, children, babies, as well as cattle...

Genocide is not a matter of playing games. Whether or not Haman is fooling himself, or trying to fool us, is a matter for us to decide.

In any case, as virtually all commentators agree, the story told in the book of Esther is a fiction. So, in all likelihood, are the stories of Exod. 17 and 1 Sam. 15. So, too, the genocide of the Canaanites in Joshua is unhistorical.

But genocide is not always a fiction. The twentieth century has shown us that. How, then, should we respond to stories that celebrate it, however innocently and however playfully? If we can't forget them, is it not up to us to reinterpret or abandon them?[26]

23. The Hebrew here, *ma'adannot*, is of uncertain meaning.

24. 1 Sam. 15.32-33.

25. According to Est. 9.13, Haman's ten sons were hanged, specifically at Esther's personal request. Fox says (1991: 224 n. 17), 'even if hostility toward Amalek was Mordecai's reason for not bowing to Haman, he did not set out to eradicate Amalek and there is nothing to suggest that this was the result'. But why else were Haman's sons executed? Laniak (1998: n. 80) asks whether the sons were killed before hanging (Heb: *talah*). In support of his suggestion is that their death is already recorded earlier in Est. 9.10. Such an act would also mirror (as Laniak notes) the fate of Saul at the hands of the Philistines.

26. Schalom Ben-Chorin urged, as Nazi persecution of the Jews was intensifying (Ben-Chorin 1938), that the book should be decanonized. Decanonization is impossible, but post-Holocaust and in the light of continuing racial hatred around the world and even within Western societies, the book sits uncomfortably on our consciences. Or it ought to. Like the memory of the British Guy Fawkes, the racial-religious hatred that it contains should disappear—perhaps impossible in this case, in which case the celebration might be quietly forgotten. Haman can be a dangerous symbol for anyone who happens to be an object of racial hatred or fear. For a more recent appreciation by a Jewish scholar of the problem of the book of Esther in a wider cultural and religious perspective, see Levenson 1976.

BIBLIOGRAPHY

General

Barbour, John D.
    1987   'Character and Characterization in Religious Autobiography', *JAAR* 55: 307-27.

Christianson, E.
    1998   *A Time to Tell: Narrative Strategies in Ecclesisastes* (JSOTSup, 280; Sheffield: Sheffield Academic Press).

Davies, Philip R.
    1995   'Male Bonding: A Tale of Two Buddies', in *idem, Whose Bible Is It Anyway?* (JSOTSup, 204; Sheffield: Sheffield Academic Press): 95-113.

Iser, Wolfgang
    1978   *The Act of Reading: A Theory of Aesthetic Response* (London: Routledge & Kegan Paul).

Moore, Stephen
    1995   'True Confessions and Weird Obsessions: Autobiographical Interventions in Literary and Biblical Studies', in Janice Capel Anderson and Jeffrey L. Staley (eds.), *Taking It Personally* (Semeia, 72; Atlanta: Scholars Press): 19-50.

Sherwood, Yvonne
    1996   *The Prostitute and the Prophet* (JSOTSup, 212; Sheffield: Sheffield Academic Press).

Smith, Morton
    1971   'Pseudepigraphy in the Israelite Literary Tradition', in K. von Fritz (ed.), *Pseudepigrapha, Pseudopythagorica, Lettres de Platon, Littérature pseudepigraphique juive*, I (Geneva: Labor et fides): 189-215.

Vermes, Geza
    1973   *Scripture and Tradition in Judaism* (Leiden: E.J. Brill).

Genesis Characters

Alter, Robert
    1981   *The Art of Biblical Narrative* (New York: Basic Books).
    1996   *Genesis: Translation and commentary* (New York: W.W. Norton).

Barfoot, James
    1988   'The Nude in Nights as Two (from Genesis XIX),' *Christianity and Literature* 37/4: 23.

Bird, Phyllis A. (ed.)
    1997   *Missing Persons and Mistaken Identities: Women and Gender in Ancient Israel* (Minneapolis: Fortress Press).

Brueggemann, Walter
    1982   *Genesis* (Atlanta: John Knox Press).
Day, Peggy L. (ed.)
    1989   *Gender and Difference in Ancient Israel* (Minneapolis: Fortress Press).
Elliott, Ralph H.
    1961   *The Message of Genesis* (Nashville: Broadman Press).
Frankel, Ellen
    1996   *The Five Books of Miriam* (New York: Putnam's Sons).
Goldin, Judah
    1977   'The Youngest Son or Where does Genesis 38 Belong?', *JBL* 96: 27-44.
Gunn, David M., and Danna Nolan Fewell
    1993   *Narrative in the Hebrew Bible* (Oxford: Oxford University Press).
Hayes, C.E.
    1995   'The Midrashic Career of the Confession of Judah (Genesis XXXVIII 26):
                Part I: The extra-canonical texts, targums and other versions', *VT* 45: 62-81.
Hewett, John H.
    1989   'Genesis 2.4b–3.31; 4.2-16; 9.20-27; 19.30-38', *Review and Expositor* 86:
                237-41.
Johnson, Marshall D.
    1969   *The Purpose of the Biblical Genealogies with Special Reference to the
                Setting of the Genealogies of Jesus* (Cambridge: Cambridge University
                Press).
Lacocque, André
    1990   *The Feminine Unconventional: Four Subversive Figures in Israel's Tradi-
                tion* (Minneapolis: Fortress Press).
Maddox, Randy L.
    1987   'Damned if You Do and Damned if You Don't: Tamar—A Feminist Fore-
                mother: Genesis 38: 6-26', *Daughters of Sarah* 13/4: 14-17.
Mathewson, Steven D.
    1989   'An Exegetical Study of Genesis 38', *Bibliotheca Sacra* 146: 373-92.
Menn, Esther Marie
    1997   *Judah and Tamar (Genesis 38) in Ancient Jewish Exegesis: Studies in
                Literary Form and Hermeneutics* (Leiden: E.J. Brill).
Rendsburg, Gary A.
    1986   'David and his Circle in Genesis XXXVIII', *VT* 36: 438-46.
Speiser, E.A.
    1964   *Genesis* (AB, 1; Garden City, NY: Doubleday).
Trible, Phyllis
    1978   *God and the Rhetoric of Sexuality* (Philadelphia: Fortress Press).
Ulanov, Ann B.
    1993   *The Female Ancestors of Christ* (Boston, MA: Shambhala).
Van der Horst, Pieter W.
    1993   'Tamar in Pseudo-Philo's Biblical History', in Athalya Brenner (ed.), *A
                Feminist Companion to Genesis* (The Feminist Companion to the Bible, 2;
                Sheffield: Sheffield Academic Press): 300-304.
Van Leeuwen, Mary S.
    1990   *Gender and Grace: Women and Men in a Changing World* (Leicester: Inter-
                Varsity Press).

Van Wolde, Ellen
    1997   'Texts In Dialogue with Texts: Intertextuality in the Ruth and Tamar Narratives', *BibInt* 5: 1-28.
Wright, George R.H.
    1982   'The Positioning of Genesis 38', *ZAW* 94: 523-29.

Raḥab

Bal, Mieke
    1985   *Narratology: Introduction to the Theory of Narrative* (Toronto: University of Toronto Press).
Bechtel, Lyn M.
    1991   'Shame as a Sanction of Social Control in Biblical Israel: Judicial, Political, and Social Shaming', *JSOT* 40: 161-77.
Bendor, S.
    1994   *The Israelite Beth 'Ab* (Jerusalem: Simor) [Hebrew].
Bird, Phyllis
    1989   'To 'Play the Harlot': An Inquiry into an Old Testament Metaphor', in Peggy L. Day (ed.), *Gender and Difference in Ancient Israel* (Minneapolis: Fortress Press): 75-94.
Blenkinsopp, Joseph
    1997   'The Family in First Temple Israel', in Perdue *et al.* 1997: 49-82.
Brenner, Athalya (ed.)
    1994   *A Feminist Companion to Samuel–Kings* (The Feminist Companion to the Bible, 5; Sheffield: Sheffield Academic Press).
Brenner, Athalya
    1997   *The Intercourse of Knowledge: On Gendering 'Love' and Desire in the Hebrew Bible* (Leiden: E.J. Brill).
Cornelius, Izak
    1997   'The Many Faces of God: Divine Images and Symbols in Ancient Near Eastern Religions', in Karel van der Toorn (ed.), *The Image and the Book: Iconic Cults, Aniconism, and the Rise of Book Religion in Israel and the Ancient Near East* (Leuven: Peeters): 21-43.
Dever, William G.
    1992   'Israel, History of (Archaeology and the Israelite "Conquest")', in *ABD*, III: 545-58.
Edelman, Diana V. (ed.)
    1995   *The Triumph of Elohim* (Kampen: Kok).
Holland, T.A.
    1992   'Jericho', in *ABD*, III: 723-37.
Klein, Lillian R.
    1995   'Honor and Shame in Esther', in A. Brenner (ed.), *A Feminist Companion to Esther, Judith and Susanna* (The Feminist Companion to the Bible, 7; Sheffield: Sheffield Academic Press): 149-75.
Lang, Bernhard
    1980   'Schule und Uterricht im alten Israel', in B. Lang (ed.), *Wie wird man Prophet in Israel?* (Düsseldorf: Patmos): 104-19.

Meyers, Carol
    1994   'Hannah and her Sacrifice: Reclaiming Female Agency', in Brenner 1994:
                93-104.
    1997   'The Family in Ancient Israel', in Perdue *et al.* 1997: 1-47.
Niditch, Susan
    1993   *War in the Hebrew Bible: A Study in the Ethics of Violence* (Oxford: Oxford
                University Press).
Perdue, L.G. *et al.*
    1997   *Families in Ancient Israel* (Louisville: Westminster/John Knox Press).
Pilch, John J.
    1997   'Family Violence in Cross-Cultural Perspective: An Approach for Feminist
                Interpreters of the Bible', in A. Brenner and Carole Fontaine (eds.), *A
                Feminist Companion to Reading the Bible: Approaches, Methods and
                Strategies* (The Feminist Companion to the Bible, 11; Sheffield: Sheffield
                Academic Press): 306-23.
Reinhartz, Adele
    1994   'Anonymous Women and the Collapse of the Monarchy: A Study in
                Narrative Technique', in Brenner 1994: 43-65.
Sternberg, M.
    1985   *The Poetics of Biblical Narrative* (Bloomington: University of Indiana
                Press).
Van der Toorn, Karel
    1989   'Female Prostitution in Payment of Vows in Ancient Israel', *JBL* 108: 93-
                205.
Yadin, Yigael
    1963   *The Art of Warfare in Biblical Lands in the Light of Archaeological Study*
                (Jerusalem: International Publishing Company).
Zakovitch, Y.
    1990   'Humor and Theology or the Successful Failure of Israelite Intelligence: A
                Literary-Folklonistic Approach to Joshua', in Susan Niditch (ed.), *Text and
                Tradition: The Hebrew Bible and Folklore* (Atlanta: Scholars Press): 75-98.

Delilah

Amit, Y.
    1992   '"The Glory of Israel does not deceive or change His mind": On the
                Reliability of Narrator and Speakers in Biblical Narrative', *Prooftexts* 12:
                201-12.
Arpaly, B.
    1998   *Masternovel: Five Essays on Temol Shilshom by S.Y. Agnon* (Tel Aviv:
                Hakibbuz Hameuchad Publishing House [Hebrew]).
Bal, M.
    1987   *Lethal Love: Feminist Literary Readings of Biblical Love Stories* (Bloom-
                ington: Indiana University Press).
Boling, R.G.
    1975   *Judges* (AB, 6a; Garden City, NY: Doubleday).

Buber, S. (ed.).
 1902   *Agadath Bereschith: Midraschische Auslegungen zum ersten Buche Mosis*
         (Krakau: Josef Fischer).
Burney, C.F.
 1970   *The Book of Judges* (London: Rivingtons; repr. New York: Ktav, 1903).
Charlesworth, J.H. (ed.)
 1985   *The Old Testament Pseudepigrapha*, II (Garden City, NY: Doubleday).
Collins, J.C. (ed.)
 1950   *John Milton's Samson Agonistes* (Oxford: Clarendon Press).
Danby, H. (trans. and ed.)
 1933   *The Mishnah* (London: Oxford University Press).
Eisenstein, J.D. (ed.)
 1928   *Ozar Midrashim: A Library of Two Hundred Minor Midrashim*, I (New
         York: Reznick, Menschel & Co.) [Hebrew].
Elitzur, Y.
 1976   *The Book of Judges* (Da'at Miqra': Jerusalem: The Rav Kook Institute)
         [Hebrew].
Epstein, I. (trans.)
 1933   *The Babylonian Talmud: Seder Nashim in Four Volumes*, III (London:
         Soncino).
Even, J.
 1968   'Represented Speech: A Concept in the Theory of Prose and its Uses in
         Hebrew Fiction', *Hasifrut* 1.1: 140-52 [Hebrew].
Fishelov, D.
 1996   'Delilah's Rhetorical Portraits', *Motar* 4: 59-64 [Hebrew].
Forshey, G.E.
 1992   *American Religious and Biblical Spectaculars* (Westport, CT: Praeger).
Goldberg, L.
 1973   'The Love of Samson', in *Muqdam Ume'uhar* (Merḥaviah: Sifriat Poalim):
         228-32 [Hebrew].
Golomb, H.
 1968   'Combined Speech: A Major Technique in the Prose of S.Y. Agnon: Its Use
         in the Story "A Different Face"', *Hasifrut* 1.2: 251-62 [Hebrew].
Gunkel, H.
 1901   *The Legends of Genesis* (trans. W.H. Carruth; Chicago: Open Court; repr;
         New York: Schocken Books, 1964).
Jabotinsky, Vladimir (Ze'ev).
 1930   *Samson* (trans. B. Krupnik; Berlin/Tel Aviv: A.Y. Shtible) [Hebrew].
Kahr, M.
 1972   'Delilah', *The Art Bulletin* 54: 282-99.
 1973   'Rembrandt and Delilah', *Art Bulletin* 55: 240-59.
Liver, J.
 1965   'Delilah', in E.L. Sukenik *et al.* (eds.), *Encyclopaedia Biblica*, II (Jerusalem:
         Bialik Institute): 656 [Hebrew].
Moore, G.F.
 1895   *Judges* (ICC; Edinburgh: T. & T. Clark; repr. Edinburgh: T. & T. Clark,
         1966).

Naveh, J.
    1968   'Nahal Șorek', in E.L. Sukenik *et al.* (eds.), *Encyclopaedia Biblica*, V (Jerusalem: Bialik Institute): 814-15 [Hebrew].

Neusner, Jacob (trans. and ed.)
    1985   *The Talmud of the Land of Israel.* XXII. *Ketubot* (Chicago: University of Chicago Press).

Noth, M.
    1966   *Die israelitischen Personennamen im Rahmen der gemeinsemitischen Namengebung* (BWANT, 10; Stuttgart: W. Kohlhammer, 1928; repr. Hildesheim: Georg Olms).

Perry, M., and M. Sternberg
    1968   'The King Through Ironic Eyes: The Narrator's Devices in the Biblical Story of David and Bathsheba and Two Excursuses on the Theory of the Narrative Text', *Hasifrut* 1.2: 263-92 [Hebrew].

Polak, F.
    1994   *Biblical Narrative: Aspects of Art and Design* (Jerusalem: Bialik Institute) [Hebrew].

Soggin, J.A.
    1981   *Judges* (OTL; London: SCM Press).

Sternberg, M.
    1987   *The Poetics of Biblical Narrative: Ideological Literature and the Drama of Reading* (Bloomington: Indiana University Press, 1987).

Tümpel, C.
    1993   'The Influence of Josephus Flavius's Antiquities of the Jews on Seventeenth-century Painting', in Weyl and Weiss-Blok 1993: 155-67 [Hebrew].

Tümpel, C. *et al*
    1991   *Het Oude Testament in de Schilderkunst van de Gouden Eeuw* (Zwolle).
    1993   'Biblical Painting in Seventeenth-Century Holland', in Weyl and Weiss-Blok 1993: 79-153 [Hebrew].

Weyl, M., and R. Weiss-Blok (eds.)
    1993   *Rembrandt's Holland* (Jerusalem: The Israel Museum).

Zakovitch, Y.
    1982   *The Life of Samson (Judges 13–16): A Literary-Critical Analysis* (Jerusalem: Magnes Press) [Hebrew].

Jezebel

Ackerman, Susan
    1999   '"And the women knead dough": The Worship of the Queen of Heaven in Sixth-Century Judah', in Alice Bach (ed.), *Women in the Hebrew Bible: A Reader* (New York: Routledge): 21-32.

Avigad, N.
    1964   'The Seal of Jezebel', *IEJ* 14: 274-76.

Bernard, Bruce
    1983   *The Bible and its Painters* (London: Orbis).

Day Lewis, Cecil
    1966   *The Eclogues, Georgics and Aeneid of Virgil* (Oxford: Oxford University Press).

Exum, J. Cheryl
    1996   *Plotted, Shot and Painted: Cultural Representations of Biblical Women* (JSOTSup, 215; Sheffield: Sheffield Academic Press).

Gaines, Janet Howe
    1999   *Music in the Old Bones: Jezebel Through the Ages* (Carbondale, IL: Southern Illinois University Press).

Herm, Gerhard
    1975   *The Phoenicians: The Purple Empire of the Ancient World* (trans. C. Hillier; London: Victor Gollancz).

Katzenstein, H. Jacob
    1997   *The History of Tyre: From the Beginning of the Second Millenium B.C.E. until the Fall of the Neo-Babylonian Empire in 539 B.C.E.* (Beer Sheva: Ben-Gurion University of the Negev Press, rev. edn).

Onions, C.T.
    1973   *The Shorter Oxford English Dictionary on Historical Principles*, I (Oxford: Oxford University Press, 3rd edn).

Pritchard, James B.
    1978   *Recovering Sarepta, A Phoenician City* (Princeton: Princeton University Press).

Hosea and Gomer

Andersen, F.I., and D.N. Freedman
    1980   *Hosea* (AB; Garden City, NY: Doubleday).

Balz-Cochois, H.
    1982a   'Gomer oder die Macht der Astarte', *EvT* 42: 37-65.
    1982b   *Gomer* (Frankfurt: Peter Lang).

Bird, P.
    1989   ' "To play the harlot" ', in P. Day (ed.), *Gender and Difference in Ancient Israel* (Minneapolis: Fortress Press): 75-94.

Brenner, Athalya (ed.)
    1995   *A Feminist Companion to the Latter Prophets* (The Feminist Companion to the Bible, 8; Sheffield: Sheffield Academic Press).

Davies, G.I.
    1992   *Hosea* (NCB; London: Marshall Pickering; Grand Rapids: Eerdmans).

Day, J.
    1980   'A Case of Inner Scriptural Interpretation', *JTS* NS 31: 309-19.

Dworkin, A.
    1981   *Pornography* (London: Women's Press).

Frymer-Kensky, T.
    1992   *In the Wake of the Goddesses* (New York: Free Press).

Janzen, J.G.
    1982   'Metaphor and Reality in Hosea 11', in W.A. Beardslee and D.J. Lull (eds.), *Old Testament Interpretation from a Process Perspective* (Semeia, 24; Chico, CA: Scholars Press): 7-44.

Keefe, A.
    1995   'The Female Body, the Body Politic and the Land', in Brenner 1995: 70-100.

Kreuzer, S.
    1989   'Gott als Mutter in Hosea 11?', *TQ* 169: 123-32.
Landy, F.
    1995a   'In the Wilderness of Speech', *BibInt* 3: 35-59.
    1995b   'Fantasy and the Displacement of Pleasure', in Brenner 1995: 146-60.
Renaud, B.
    1983   'Osée 1–3: Analyse diachronique et lecture synchronique', *RSR* 57: 249-60.
Schmitt, J.J.
    1989   'The Wife of God in Hosea 2', *BR* 34: 5-18.
Schüngel-Straumann, H.
    1986   'Gott als Mutter in Hosea 11', *TQ* 166: 119-34; ET 'God as Mother in Hosea
                11', in Brenner 1995: 194-218.
Setel, T.D.
    1986   'Prophets and Pornography', in L.M. Russell (ed.), *Feminist Interpretation
                of the Bible* (Oxford: Basil Blackwell; Philadelphia: Westminster Press): 86-
                95.
Unterman, J.
    1982   'Repentance and Redemption in Hosea', in K.H. Richards (ed.), *Society of
                Biblical Literature 1982 Seminar Papers* (SBLSP, 21; Chico, CA: Scholars
                Press): 541-50.
Van Dijk-Hemmes, F.
    1989   'The Imagination of Power and the Power of Imagination', *JSOT* 44: 75-88
                (reprinted in A. Brenner [ed.], *A Feminist Companion to the Song of Songs*
                [The Feminist Companion to the Bible, 1; Sheffield: Sheffield Academic
                Press, 1993]: 156-70).
Wacker, Marie-Therese
    1995   'Traces of the Goddess in the Book of Hosea', in Brenner 1995: 219-41.
    1996   *Figurationen des weiblichen im Hosea-Buch* (Freiburg: Herder).
Wolff, H.W.
    1974   *Hosea* (Hermeneia; Philadelphia: Fortress Press).

Haman

Beal, Timothy K.
    1997   *The Book of Hiding: Gender, Ethnicity, Annihilation and Esther* (London:
                Routledge).
Ben-Chorin, Schalom
    1938   *Kritik des Esther-Buches* (Jerusalem).
Craig, Kenneth
    1995   *Reading Esther: A Case for the Literary Carnivalesque* (Literary Currents in
                Biblical Interpretation; Louisville: Westminster/John Knox Press).
Fox, Michael V.
    1991   *Character and Ideology in the Book of Esther* (Columbia, SC: University of
                South Carolina Press).
Fretz, Mark J.
    1992   'Agagite (person)', in *ABD*, I: 89-90.

Laniak, Timothy S.
    1998   *Shame and Honor in the Book of Esther* (SBLDS, 165; Atlanta: Scholars Press).
Levenson, Jon D.
    1976   'The Scroll of Esther in Ecumenical Perspective', *JES* 12: 440-51.
    1997   *Esther: A Commentary* (OTL; Louisville: Westminster/John Knox Press; London: SCM Press).
Magonet, J.
    1992   *Bible Lives* (London: SCM Press): 80-88.
Stolper, Matthew W.
    1992   'Murashû, Archive of', in *ABD*, IV: 927-28.
Zadok, Ran
    1979   *The Jews in Babylonia in the Chaldean and Achaemenid Periods in the Light of the Babylonian Sources* (Haifa: University of Haifa).
    1984   'On the Historical Background of the Book of Esther', *Biblische Notizen* 24: 18-23.

INDEXES

INDEX OF REFERENCES

BIBLE

INDEX OF AUTHORS